The Fear of Life And the Life Within Fear

The Fear of Life And the Life Within Fear
Stories from the World of Hypnosis

Published by Spines
ISBN: 979-8-90001-198-1

Spines

The Fear of Life And the Life Within Fear

Stories from the World of Hypnosis

Dr. Ali Badarni

Contents

Dedication

Dedicated to the memory of my brother, Naji Badarni, may he rest in peace, who was my friend, a mentor, and a man with a giving heart.

AUTHOR'S FOREWORD

> There is no hope without fear, and no fear that does not contain hope
>
> — BARUCH SPINOZA

Throughout our lives, each of us encounters different people who impact us to varying degrees.

Some have been present in our lives and may have caused us harm, yet fulfilled their mission and departed, thereby strengthening our immune system.

Some are present in our lives, greeting us with smiles, who cause our eyes to shine when we meet them. But we must understand that one day their mission will end, and they will depart.

Things have happened and continue to happen one after the other, all arriving to tell us something, sometimes with a slap and sometimes with a hug, guiding us and illuminating our path even further.

There is no emptiness in this world, and I am one with this world.

For nearly thirty years, I have met with thousands of people who came to me for therapy and sought help; each opened the confines of their heart to me, each a universe unto themselves. I was present with each of them at every moment of their sessions, and many times even afterwards. Some visited me in my dreams, while others shared moments of both joy and sorrow with me.

Each had an impact on me.

In this book, I recount the stories of eight of them, eight heroes through whom I confronted my own fears and past traumas, and with their help, lovingly healed many wounds that had remained open for many years.

I am grateful to them.

Every story in this book is based on several real individuals whom I merged into a single character and gave a name.

Each one of you may see yourself in every story, and it is also possible that you will find a part of yourself in stories such as "The Lady" or "His name is Saeed (which means "happy") and he's anxious all the time" or "Dr. Ayman" among others. Sometimes the reader will find themselves in the story because the hero resembles them, leading them to identify, react to their emotions, grieve in their sorrow, rejoice in their happiness, and draw lessons from the therapeutic journey. Other times, they may think that the story is about them. Each one of us is present in all these stories, sometimes as the central character and sometimes as a secondary one.

I would like to thank the book's other heroes, the ones behind the scenes who are not directly mentioned, the heroes who supported me and accompanied me throughout the writing process of this book, those who believed that a new creation was about to emerge into the world. These heroes are kindred spirits who were curious, sought explanations, smiled, and provided me with a strong safety net.

My gratitude also goes to my unique artistic friend, Amal Murkus, who encouraged me to publish this book in Hebrew, and to the amazing translator Bruria Horowitz, who embraced the challenge of fulfilling this dream and took on the translation with love, readiness, and goodwill, without any conditions.

I also thank Dr. Tzachi Arnon, former chair of the Israel Hypnosis Association, for his professional observations regarding the theoretical first part of this book.

And of course, a special thanks to my dear family: to Sawsan and Lydia, my daughters, to my son George, and my partner Maria, for their support, each in their own unique way.

I place this creation, which materialized with the arrival of my beloved granddaughter Layla, and present it before you. Through it, you will become acquainted with hypnosis and understand that we experience it every day. You will likely identify with the heroes of the stories and feel that the events described reflect a reality shared by many of us.

I wish you an enjoyable read.

Ali.

Σ

Part One

Longing and the Beginning

It was in the spring of 1988.

In one of the cobblestoned alleys in the historic neighborhood at the center of Moscow, more precisely on Taganskaya Street, I had my first encounter with hypnosis.

The snow, which had started falling in October of the previous year, had ceased. Warm, genuine rays replaced the false beams sent by the sun during the past months. Small patches of unthawed snow-covered parts of the areas between trees scattered everywhere along the streets, and the melting snow water trickled into small puddles along the roads, gently flowing into the drainage ditches.

On a sunny afternoon, I entered through a dark ground-level corridor into the place I had been seeking. It was an old two-story building built in the nineteenth century, perhaps even earlier. The building had a tiled roof whose color had changed over time due to the weather. The door I opened creaked and disrupted the silence that reigned within the building. Old marble stairs leading to the upper floor were worn in the center due to the historic friction of countless feet that had traversed them over the years. The tranquility of the second floor was broken by sunlight streaming through one of the room's windows into the narrow, dark corridor, serving as my guide.

Faint whispers reached my ears from that room. Six people sat in an informal, disorganized circle in the middle of the room, waiting for the meeting to begin. One female doctor sat between two of her male colleagues, while the rest were bearded men, tall and stout. The youngest among them was in his fifties. Their faces bore a serious and stern expression. I later understood that they were involved in parapsychology and mediumship.

As I entered, they cast curious glances at me. I greeted them with my spontaneous, youthful smile and hailed them in Russian.

Perhaps it was my youthful appearance, along with my green Adidas sports shirt and jeans, that initially caught their attention; however, when they heard my unfamiliar accent in Russian, they realized that I had come from afar.

I joined them, becoming the seventh member of the group.

I was twenty-four years old at the time, a third-year student in the Faculty of Psychology at Moscow State University, named after its founder, Mikhail Lomonosov.

The Faculty of Psychology is also located in the heart of

Moscow, in one of the historic buildings of Moscow State University that was built in 1755 and is still in use today.

The best way for me to reach the Faculty of Psychology was by subway, the metro. I rode it until the "Marx Avenue" station, whose name was changed after the collapse of the Soviet Union to "Okhotny Riad." After exiting the last carriage of the train arriving from the southwest—where I lived on Virandsky Avenue—and climbing the stairs up to the street, some dozens of meters to the left, one can see the Red Square, the Kremlin, and the Historical Museum. In the background stand the Moscow Hotel and the Duma House (the legislative building), and behind them the famous Bolshoi Theatre. In the front, about two hundred meters away, is the Faculty of Journalism, at the center of whose square stands a large statue of Mikhail Lomonosov, casting a constant gaze toward the Hall opposite it, which houses exhibitions of paintings by renowned artists.

When you turn right after getting off the train, you enter Gorky Street (now called Tverstaya).

"Tver", to which the name refers, is one of the historic cities to which this street leads. It is located on the bank of the Volga River, along the route that connects Moscow to Saint Petersburg (which was called Leningrad and, before that, Petrograd) and is considered one of the most important cultural centers in Russia. It was founded in 1135, and from the thirteenth through the fourteenth century, it was the largest hub of the national liberation movement from the Tatar yoke.

When you walk a few meters along Tverskaya Street and

turn left, you see directly opposite the Faculty of Psychology. It is an old four-story building painted in two timeless colors —white and a dark yellow resembling beige.

As for Mikhail Lomonosov, after whom Moscow State University is named, he was born in 1711 to a simple peasant family in northern Russia. As a child of limited means, he taught himself to read, write, master grammar, and study mathematics without the help of teachers.

When he was a youth, he ran away from his father's home to seek knowledge in distant Moscow, which he reached after walking more than one thousand three hundred kilometers. There, he was admitted to the Academy of Latin and Greek Sciences, and after completing his studies, he was sent to Germany, where he learned from the foremost German and Dutch instructors.

After his return to Russia, he began his scientific work at the Academy of Sciences in the Russian capital and spearheaded a reform of the education system. All his endeavors were devoted to ensuring the right to education for the impoverished segments of society.

Lomonosov founded the first chemistry laboratory in Russia, where he conducted numerous physical experiments. He also researched Russian history. He is credited with reviving the ancient art of mosaic and introducing it to Russia, in addition to proposing and founding Russia's first university in Moscow.

It is difficult to find any scientific subject to which Lomonosov did not contribute. He authored the book "Selected Chapters in Rhetoric," which became a primary authoritative source in world literature, laid the foundations for physical chemistry, and invented many optical instruments, including telescopes that the world used to study the planet Venus. One of his most fascinating studies is the one concerning the theory of heat generation resulting from the movement of particles.

Lomonosov passed away at the age of fifty-three.

Along the route between the "Marx Avenue" train station and the Faculty of Psychology—which had been an integral part of my daily routine, morning and evening, for several years—a small notice on one of the billboards scattered along the street caught my attention, inviting those interested to study and experience hypnosis.

Since hypnosis had fascinated me since childhood and was the main motivation for my study of psychology, I felt that this notice was meant for me personally, for there are no coincidences in life; events unfold with wisdom, and someone is orchestrating them.

At least, that was my belief then, and it still is.

The study and practice of hypnosis were confined to a few groups in a rather unspoken and even illegal manner in some places. Naturally, they were not included in the academic curriculum, and that remains the case even today.

With that unique, one-of-a-kind group I met there, on Taganskaya Street on the second floor of one of the old buildings, I studied and practiced hypnosis for five consecutive days from the afternoon until the late evening hours.

That was traditional hypnosis, characterized by a "command and control" approach—the demonstration of authoritarianism and the delivery of uncompromising commands and direct suggestions in a loud, sharp tone.

It was an enjoyable experience, for a world I had longed to know revealed itself to me, both scientifically and practically. I experimented with hypnosis and applied it to my group members, and in turn, they applied it to me. I understood what happens in the brain during hypnosis and discovered the easiest and most effective way to induce a hypnotic trance in a person. I also learned how one might extract secrets from a person during a normal night's sleep, but I never put that into practice—not on anyone, not even on Maria, my classmate back then and my wife today. Although I was very curious and eager, I did not do it!

After that experience, many long years passed during which I engaged in hypnosis only in its simplest forms—more precisely, practicing various relaxation techniques and guided imagery. After some time, I became acquainted with a different type of hypnosis, the kind attributed to Milton Erickson.

We will later delve into the persona of this scientist, who is considered the spiritual father of permissive hypnosis in the twentieth century.

Chapter 1

What is hypnosis?

In general, hypnosis can be described as an interaction between two or more people, where one person is the hypnotist and the other(s) are the hypnotized. The hypnotist gives verbal instructions, either orally or through gestures, and the hypnotized person carries them out.

According to the Israel Hypnosis Association[1], of which I am a member, "hypnosis is a state in which a person harnesses their ability to concentrate in order to turn their attention inward. In a state of hypnosis, one permits oneself to direct most of one's attention and resources in order to bring about a physical or mental change, to establish a more effective connection with the subconscious, or to improve the communication system between the brain and the body. Any state in which we focus the majority of our concentration on a single goal, as if 'ignoring' everything else around, possesses the characteristics of a hypnotic state..."

Hypnosis has many definitions. What is common to all these definitions is the description of hypnosis as an altered state of consciousness, in which the usual rational part is at rest and the intuitive, subconscious part becomes more accessible and active. Through this "altered state of consciousness," hidden phenomena from a person's inner, unconscious world can be evoked by a series of suggestions (hints or proposals). It is a complex therapeutic method through which behavioral, mental, cognitive, emotional, and even physical changes can be induced.

In hypnosis, the mental control mechanisms and conscious awareness are bypassed, while simultaneously evoking and intensifying primary experiences, emotions, and sensations in various domains such as vision, hearing, and smell. It is a direct way to access the inner, unconscious world.

Stored within the unconscious are repressed memories, painful experiences, frustrations, and traumas that a person has endured, transferred through various defense mechanisms activated to maintain mental health. The unconscious also harbors an enormous amount of information, emotions, and sensations that a person has either repressed or couldn't process. It is here, in particular, that the causes of many psychological problems lie; it is here that the solutions to many ailments—which manifest as various physical diseases—are especially found; and it is here that hypnosis is within reach as a means to treat them. After all, hypnosis is a form of ordinary, short-term psychological treatment compared to other therapies, and it possesses greater power due to its direct connection with the unconscious.

The unconscious is rightfully considered a compliant companion that operates covertly and sends its messages through various psychological, physical, and behavioral signs and symptoms. It does so to alert us that something is not right, or that there is a flaw in the course of our lives, necessitating some action to correct it. It sends us emotional messages—such as feelings of fear, anxiety, anger, and more—so that we may take care of ourselves and revisit the pages stored within it to rearrange them anew.

Hypnosis is a wonderful tool for establishing a connection with the unconscious in order to harness our full human potential. It is a tool that can be used to improve the quality of life and the mental health of each one of us, for through self-hypnosis, one can instill positive suggestions, cope with stress, overcome difficulties, and develop advanced and responsible ways of thinking.

One of the common myths regarding hypnosis is the notion of "loss of control." Some mistakenly believe that the practitioner controls the hypnotized individual during hypnosis, giving them commands and causing them to perform actions that they would not normally undertake. This idea, of course, is fundamentally flawed, as it is impossible—even in hypnosis—to force someone to do things they would never agree to due to their conscience, values, and principles. Any such attempt by the practitioner would undoubtedly be met by an inner critic that is constantly on guard, drawing the person's attention and rousing them when necessary. This inner critic, of course, varies from person to person and adheres to their conscience and personal values, as mentioned above.

The practitioner of hypnosis is the companion who

accompanies the individual. He or she guides and directs the person toward the goal he aspires to reach, just as Erickson did with the horse. The unconscious is the part that knows one's true inclination and leads the person to the realm of their desire in order to address their problem. Sometimes this requires deep hypnosis, and sometimes it is sufficient for the person to be in a state of light hypnosis, as the success of the treatment does not depend on the depth of the hypnotic state at all.

There is almost unanimous agreement among practitioners of hypnosis that children possess a higher capacity and readiness to respond to suggestions and enter a state of hypnotic trance, due to several factors such as their vivid imagination, their limited verbal reasoning, their desire to experience new things, and their enthusiasm for so-called "magic" tricks.

As for adults, special methods known as "induction" have been developed to help them enter a state of hypnosis.

ACCELERATING THE PROCESS OF ENTERING HYPNOSIS — HYPNOTIC INDUCTION

There are several ways to enter a state of hypnosis. This requires measured steps that are predetermined with the individual. For example, one assesses which of their sensory channels are strongest — whether it is their sense of hearing or sight, their verbal language or visual imagination, and so on.

There are countless diverse tools used for this purpose. Certain tools may be employed, such as a pendulum (swinging device) for focusing the eyes, a gong for focusing the hearing, and a metronome for focusing both sight and sound together. One can also use the verbal–auditory channel through stories or imagination and relaxation. In fact, anything present in the treatment room can be used, without delving into further details, so as not to exceed what the law permits. However, I wish to emphasize that all these means require skills, professionalism, and extensive experience.

Hypnotic induction and the steps aimed at achieving relaxation can be carried out actively, for example: "Close your eyes, squeeze your palms with all the strength you can so that they become two fists... Squeeze harder... More... Even more... And now release them... Relax them all at once... Your eyes are closed... Your breathing is calm." It can also be done passively (Passive), for example: "Sit comfortably... Let go of your hands and feet... Inhale air and exhale it... A calm inhalation and slow exhalation... Imagine the air entering your body through your nose, passing through your trachea and reaching your lungs... from there the oxygen is carried to all your organs... to every single cell... Imagine for yourself the process of gas exchange... and the return of the blood to the lungs loaded with carbon dioxide... Now it exits the body through your mouth... slowly and serenely... Breathe a calm, slow breath... Now I will count to ten... each number representing a deeper level leading to greater relaxation..."

Once the therapist notices signs from the patient that indicate their entry into the first stage of hypnosis, he or she begins the work of strengthening and deepening the hypnosis more and more through direct suggestions and other methods to initiate the treatment.

There are four stages of hypnosis: a state of relaxation and imagination, light hypnosis, moderate hypnosis accompanied, for example, by mild numbness in parts of the body and amnesia (oblivion), and deep hypnosis, which is accompanied by hallucinations, amnesia, and the possibility to regress in age in order to deal with a trauma that occurred in the past or other symptoms. The therapist determines, in coordination with the patient, the appropriate stage for treatment according to the patient's personality and characteristics, as well as the goal of the therapy.

Some people agree to treatment through hypnosis but exhibit hidden resistance. For example, they may open their eyes and then close them, or their eyelids may continue to tremble, and sometimes various other symptoms appear. To hypnotize these individuals, it is necessary to use other means, and it is the hypnotist who determines these, after monitoring their resistance during the initial meetings (Intake) or even during the hypnotic induction.

Other situations may arise in which the hypnotized person refuses to exit the hypnotic state and return to reality. These situations require special attention from the therapist to examine the reasons for the person's "desire" to remain in a hypnotic state. Generally, these situations can be handled without particular difficulty, provided that the therapist is well-skilled and experienced in this matter.

There is, of course, the possibility of teaching self-hypnosis so that the patient may use it to maintain continuity in treatment between sessions. Self-hypnosis is taught during hypnosis therapy sessions, as well as through the use of posthypnotic suggestions. These are suggestions that come into effect after the hypnosis session has ended.

Self-hypnosis must be tailored individually for each person, and in order to use it, its goals must be defined in advance, and certain conditions must be met. First and foremost, it is necessary to establish the appropriate circumstances under which it will take place, the suitable location and time, and more. Then, the person must be taught how to exit the hypnotic state or the "signal" by which he will exit, and afterwards be taught again how to enter hypnosis:

"From now on, it will be easy for you to enter a state of hypnosis once you sit quietly and calmly, achieve relaxation, and maintain continuity in accordance with the method of entering hypnosis that you have chosen. You can only reach this state if certain conditions are met: when you decide and desire it, and provided that the time and place are appropriate. Only if these conditions are met will you be able to enter the state of hypnosis, and then you will be able to follow all the instructions we follow here. When you are in a state of complete relaxation, you can immediately exit the hypnosis if there is a psychological or physical need, or in any other situation. To exit the hypnosis, simply open and close your hand three times and open your eyes."

It is very important to pay attention to the duration for which a person remains in a state of self-hypnosis. One should remain in this state once or twice a day for no more than twenty minutes, or several times a day, for no more than half an hour in total.

Chapter 2

The Changes Occurring During Hypnosis

During hypnosis, mental-cognitive, psychological, physical, and behavioral changes occur.

Mental-cognitive changes: self-control mechanisms weaken, thinking becomes more primitive and associative, analytical thinking diminishes, the rate of thought slows, and logical reasoning becomes disrupted. Primary, tangible, concrete ways of thinking emerge, relying on the senses of sight, hearing, smell, and touch. Attention becomes internally focused, and there is a sensory disconnection from the external world. The perception of time becomes distorted and warped, and hypnosis may generally be accompanied by hallucinations and seeing things that do not exist.

- Psychological changes: we notice an inner calm and tranquility, and a focus on deep emotions. Emotional responses may appear, which can also be initiated and suggested by the hypnotist-therapist.

- Physiological changes: an increase in activity in the right hemisphere of the brain, the appearance of alpha waves, a decrease in heart rate, blood pressure, and breathing rate, a reduction in the activity of the sympathetic nervous system (which operates in states of stress and tension), and an increase in the parasympathetic nervous system (which accompanies states of relaxation and mental tranquility).
- Behavioral changes: we notice a lack of movement accompanied by quiet and overall relaxation.

During hypnosis, the person disconnects from the surrounding reality and deals with internal stimuli in a way that is not possible in real life. It is similar to how one deals with situations and events revealed in a dream, which are experienced as if they were reality.

Each of you has surely experienced something while watching a movie that you loved or identified with its hero. We see the viewer reacting emotionally, suffering from a sad ending, becoming angry at an event that harmed the hero, and even sometimes speaking to him and warning him of the betrayal by one of the characters or of a conspiracy being woven against him. All of this while he knows, deep in his heart and in his consciousness, that what he sees is nothing but a movie, and that there is no real conspiracy, no murder, or any other real phenomenon.

For clarification, let me say that if each of you were to set up a camera and document your behavior while watching a decisive football match for the team you support, you would undoubtedly be very surprised, perhaps barely recognizing yourself, and burst into laughter when you saw yourself hypnotized and reacting strangely to what you see on the television screen.

The fundamental characteristic of therapeutic hypnosis is the use of suggestions and directing the person to a safe place, so that they may reach it and find inner peace and a high level of mental and physical health.

Chapter 3

Suggestions and Their Influence on Others

Suggestion is a psychological process whose purpose is to transmit a certain thought to another person in an indirect manner, without going through their conscious mind and intellectual control mechanisms. Control is indeed reduced, but it is not eliminated; therefore, one cannot offer a suggestion that contradicts someone's values and conscience. Suggestions can bring about changes in a person's behavior, thoughts, sensations, emotions, opinions, and beliefs. To achieve this goal, verbal or motor means are used, such as changes in the tone of voice, music, and more.

To explain and simplify the concept of suggestion, let us present, for example, a situation that each of us encounters daily. When we meet a person and he extends his hand to us without saying a word, we usually respond by extending our hand and shaking their hand. That person did not ask us to extend our hand; all he did was a simple gesture that influenced us, resulting in us extending our hand and shaking his hand. In other words, through the suggestion executed via a motor gesture, our behavior was elicited even without our being aware of it.

Another example of suggestion: A mother asks her son in the morning if he would like her to make him a sandwich with peanut butter, or a sandwich with an omelette for school – while the child actually wants to have a chocolate sandwich every day or does not want to take any food to school at all. Or she asks him if he prefers to wear the blue coat or the red one, while the child refuses to wear a coat at all when it is cold outside. Or when one of us gives our interlocutor the right of choice by asking him when he would like to meet, today at noon or tomorrow morning. In all these situations, suggestion is performed on the interlocutor by ensuring that they have no alternative other than the two options offered, and they must only choose between them.

Suggestions can be negative or positive. It depends, in fact, on the resulting behavioral, psychological, physical, and cognitive outcome experienced by the person to whom the suggestion is given.

Suggestion is employed, for example, when the doctor tells a patient: "Take this medication, and if your condition does not improve within a week, come back to see me." This, in itself, is a suggestion for a lack of improvement among people with a psychosomatic (mind–body) background, or those who belong to the group of suggestible individuals or who have a good readiness for hypnosis. One might say, for example: "Take this medication and let me know in a week how much it helped you." Here, the suggestion is for improvement resulting from this medication. Certainly, there are certain situations in which the psychological factor influenced by suggestion is secondary to the physical illness from which the person suffers. In this case, suggestion has only a limited role.

In this context, the effect of placebo drugs on certain patients can also be explained. It is the suggestion—and only the suggestion—that is responsible for the improvement observed in that group of people. In many cases, it is an unconscious self-induced suggestion when it comes to placebos.

Nevertheless, even in this case, the power of verbal suggestion outweighs the effectiveness of the placebo.

A study was conducted among a group of people who complained of certain physical symptoms, and no objectively diagnosed organic medical cause was found for their condition.[2] The group, which included two hundred people, was divided into four smaller groups, and the doctor undertook their treatment all together.

The doctor told each member of the first group: "In a few days, you will feel an improvement in your condition. No treatment is necessary."

To the members of the second group, he said: "In a few days, you will feel an improvement in your condition thanks to the treatment I will give you," and he gave the members of that group a placebo.

To the members of the third group, he said, "I have no idea what is wrong with you, so I will not give you any treatment. Return to see me in a few days if there is no change in your condition."

And to the members of the fourth group, he said: "I have no idea what is wrong with you, so I do not know how to treat you. Return to see me in a few days if there is no change in your condition," and he gave each of them a placebo.

After two weeks, it turned out that 64% of the members of the first two groups, the first and second, reported an improvement in their condition, compared to 39% of the members of the other two groups, the third and fourth. In other words, there was no difference between the two groups, whose members took the placebo and those whose members took no medication at all. This indicates that the effect of verbal suggestion was stronger than that of the placebo.

Suggestion is also implemented in the conclusion written by a cardiologist stating that "there is no significant problem with the heart" for a person who was healthy until the examination. This is a negative suggestion implying that there is a problem in the functioning of the heart (even if it is not significant, it still exists). One can observe a positive suggestion in a case where such a statement is made to a person suffering from chronic heart disease or some other serious issue with their cardiac functions.

The statement "there is no significant problem" is a kind of suggestion that led the first group to believe that a problem exists, while for the second group, it led them to believe that there is no problem. This is the situation when a patient is transferred to a hospital by an ambulance that activates its siren. If the patient is in a severe condition, the siren functions as a positive suggestion, since it makes him think that the temporary treatment they are receiving is fast-acting. Conversely, for a patient whose condition is not serious and who does not appear to be in danger, the siren represents a negative suggestion, because it indicates an acute situation requiring treatment.

Suggestion is also employed when we write in the examination summary phrases such as: "An urgent examination must be carried out," or when we say to the patient—in order to encourage and try to persuade them to undergo an important heart surgery—that there is a "ticking bomb" in their chest and that they should have a catheterization or open-heart surgery as soon as possible.

Imagine what a patient feels who is holding a medical report stating that there is a "ticking bomb" in his chest, while they are waiting for heart surgery, yet the scheduled date for the surgery is in a month or some other short period. Indeed, there is a danger that the patient will not be able to bear the wait, and that the unintentional suggestions made to them will lead to negative outcomes even before the operation.

Suggestion is also used when we tell a child: "Don't worry" or "Don't be afraid." In doing so, we are in fact causing the child to think that they must worry and be afraid. These words can be replaced with other, positive phrases, such as: "You are strong," "You are confident," "I admire your courage," and so on.

The unconscious does not understand negation. We must address it in the language of affirmation in order to evoke positive behavior or emotion.

"Do not imagine a white dog at this moment", "Do not imagine a large football field filled with a crowd that never stops cheering at the end of the World Cup." Did you succeed? Did you manage not to imagine? Obviously, you did imagine—or most of you did—even though I asked you not to.

Generally, we tend to rely on suggestions when we are searching for the negative. As if we say, for example, "What hurts you?" instead of asking "How are you?" or "Tell me how you feel today." If we emphasize the negative, we will have to identify that "negative" aspect—even if it is minimal—and we will focus on it. This prevents us from seeing the "good" or the "positive." Conversely, if we emphasize the positive and inquire about it, even if it is simple and small, the person will focus on it and flourish.

Words have tremendous power and influence over reality.

The Japanese scientist, Masaru Emoto (1999), demonstrated that language affects water.[3] Using a very high-resolution microscopic camera, he managed to photograph various forms of frozen water crystals as they "react" to words. For example, frozen water crystals form into vibrant and dazzling snowflake shapes when words of love are whispered to the water. Conversely, in murky water—or water that has been exposed to negative thoughts—imperfect and asymmetrical forms with very pale colors appear. Music, images, and even words written on a page also influence water, as reflected in the way water responds. Emoto believed that this response could be harnessed in treating a person and their environment through a deliberate expression of love, good intentions, and various positive emotions.

Suggestion reaches students during an exam through the teacher's behavior, as well as through his glances, smile or scowling face, sighs, breaths, tone of voice, composure, or nervousness. All of these are messages and suggestions that reach the student and affect his mental and emotional state.

One of the teachers told me that, in order to encourage his students to study, he used to say to them: "The exam will be very difficult. Anyone who does not prepare for it as required will encounter great difficulty and may fail."

The teacher's intention was positive. He wanted to encourage his students to study and thoughtfully prepare for the exam. As we can see, the emphasis here is on the words: "very difficult," "does not prepare," "may fail."

What message are we sending to the unconscious of these students through this suggestion?

Even though it has been argued that the unconscious does not understand negative language — and that one cannot jest with it — we inadvertently sent the students a message that is not the preferred one. All that can be said about it is that "it is not enough to help them" achieve the required outcomes.

So what is the alternative?

The alternative is as follows:

"The exam will be easy, and even very easy for students who prepare for it as required. Anyone who studies properly will succeed." Does this in any way diminish the students' motivation to study?

A woman came to me and complained that she bursts into tears every time she speaks about herself in front of others, whether before one person or in front of a group. "I want to be strong," she said.

The woman is in her late thirties, a widow for over ten years. She has four children, the eldest of whom studies medicine in England after receiving a scholarship for his academic excellence and volunteer community work. The second son also received a scholarship due to his outstanding academic performance at an American university. Her other two sons are high school students, both among the top of their classes. In addition, the woman has long served as the deputy branch manager at a bank in her village.

Despite all this, she complains that she bursts into tears in front of others because of a weak personality and low self-confidence. Strange, isn't it?

The oddity, for those who have not yet "grasped" the idea, is the stark contrast between what is apparent and what is hidden—the gap between this woman's power as manifested in her work at the bank and her ability to raise successful children on her own, and what she feels inside about herself, perceiving herself as "weak."

This woman repeatedly "convinced" herself that "crying means weakness," and she does not want to appear weak or be weak. When crying becomes associated with weakness, it is difficult to break this cycle as it tightens further. I had to work with her, of course, on changing and redefining the concepts and thought patterns engraved in her mind, which affected her emotions and caused her to burst into tears, a reaction that in turn led to an additional feeling of weakness, lack of self-confidence, low self-esteem, and so on.

Does crying truly mean weakness? And what is the meaning of the tears that stream after a bout of rolling laughter?

What does she instill in her consciousness and tell herself before she speaks about herself to others? What happens when she cries?

These and other questions serve as guiding queries meant to change the negative thought patterns and perceptions that reinforce the behavior she wishes to overcome—her crying outbursts.

Alongside this work, I proposed that she change this "negative self-hypnosis" and replace it with a positive one, by instilling new thoughts and suggestions, such as "I am strong, and I love myself in every situation, even when I cry."

She chose that phrase on her own after a therapy session.

A month later, the woman returned to me and recounted two separate events: in one, she confronted an inspector at a government office, and in the other, she confronted the regional manager at a bank during a meeting, after expressing her opposition to the bank's policy toward its clients.

Her friends told her that she was "changing." When I asked her the reason for this change, she said, "I don't know."

What is important is that the suggestions seeped into her unconscious and began to instigate changes in her attitudes and perceptions. As a result, her behavior naturally changed.

When we examine the matter and delve into it based on analytical and dynamic orientations in psychology, we must concentrate more on her past experiences, her childhood, her coping with the loss of her husband, the psychological defense mechanisms at work within her, her internal struggles, the role of the "self" in resolving them, and so on.

However, I believed that cognitive-behavioral therapy combined with hypnosis—relying on a change in self-suggestions—is the ideal and most succinct method for treating her crying outbursts, which had long instilled in her consciousness that she possesses a "weak personality."

We use suggestions on a daily basis, even without being aware of it, whether we are the ones giving the suggestion ourselves or receiving it from others. I will not delve into the subject of marketing and advertising here. Still, I would like to note that the fundamental basis of all marketing activities is suggestion, and we, as consumers, only truly wake up when our credit card bill arrives.

These are, of course, familiar situations that we encounter every day. The suggestions used for therapeutic purposes run much deeper than those mentioned above and must be tailored to the goals and the individual's therapeutic plan.

Through suggestions made during the hypnotic therapeutic process, we can change people's attitudes, thoughts, opinions, feelings, and beliefs. We can induce both sensory and physical changes. As with any suggestion, a person may accept it in its entirety, accept only a part of it, or even refuse it. However, under the influence of hypnosis, this process takes on a different form, as the willingness to accept the suggestion is greater. For example, a suggestion can lower the level of pain for someone complaining of chronic or temporary pain, reduce the blood pressure of someone suffering from hypertension, and decrease the level of anxiety or fear of something.

A person's response to suggestions is not voluntary. For example, when a suggestion makes someone feel that their hand is heavy, it gradually begins to drop without any intervention on their part, as if it were an entirely separate entity. In this case, the movement of the hand becomes detached from personal consciousness. It is also possible to reinforce suggestions by combining them with the sense of sight or other senses. For instance, consider the heavy hand. A person's response will be stronger and quicker if we tell them that their hand is tied with a heavy iron chain or that it is carrying a heavy iron ball. Or, for example, to evoke numbness in the hand, one might imagine a lump of snow in the area designated for numbness.

Suggestions can be divided into two types according to the manner in which they are given. Some people respond more to the "authoritative" approach, the commanding and direct style, such as the statement: "Your hand is beginning to drop now." Others respond more favorably to the permissive, facilitative, and relaxed style (the method of Milton Erickson), for example: "Just allow your hand to drop at the pace it wishes." The permissive and relaxed form of suggestion is suitable for certain individuals, especially those who find it difficult to be hypnotized. In such cases, one should focus on the desired action indirectly; for instance, on the suggestion given at that moment that is not solely related to the hand dropping, but also to the pace at which the hand chooses to drop. In other words, there is no mention whatsoever of "the hand dropping," since there is no resistance to it and no room for debate, only a focus on the pace of its descent. And thus we see that these individuals focused on a secondary matter while ignoring the primary objective—the dropping of the hand, which, after all, is the goal.

Suggestions can be indirect and implicit, for example,

the statement: "Try to ensure that your hand doesn't drop quickly," or "Do not feel complete relaxation until your hand touches your thigh." Here too, the focus shifts to another matter—namely, avoiding a rapid drop of the hand and concentrating on its slow descent or conditioning complete relaxation on the hand touching the thigh after it drops. In both cases, without a doubt, the hand will drop.

The influence of suggestions is conditioned by several factors, the most important of which is age. It is known that children are much more receptive to hypnosis and the influence of suggestions due to their great capacity for imagination. Up to the age of 10–12, suggestions carry tremendous power, which diminishes as one grows older. In general, women are more receptive than men to suggestions.

People respond to suggestions at varying levels. They can be classified according to different scales of suggestibility, such as the Harvard Group Scale of Hypnotic Susceptibility (HGSHS: Harvard Group Scale of Hypnotic Susceptibility) and the Stanford Hypnotic Susceptibility Scale (SHSS: Stanford Hypnotic Susceptibility Scale).

Most people are easily influenced by suggestions (suggestible), but there are also those with low suggestibility.

Therapeutic suggestions are given before the actual start of treatment—that is, before the person enters the treatment room—for example, during the telephone call to schedule a therapy session, or while waiting for the appointment. Likewise, suggestions are given during the session so that their effect begins after leaving the clinic. These suggestions are called "post-hypnotic suggestions" or "future suggestions": "When you return to your 'normal' state and leave here, that wonderful feeling of calm and serenity will continue to accompany you... It will appear every time you need it... You might be surprised by the tranquility and strength you will feel when you enter the testing room... A slight smile may appear on your face when you receive the test form... You may even feel uplifted as you look into the eyes of your fellow students.".

Chapter 4

Trance and Hypnosis

Trance is one of the states of hypnosis and one of its stages. It is a state of consciousness that directs attention inward, toward thoughts and feelings. It is a state of alertness and of focusing on the person's inner world. When a person is in a trance, they remain alert and self-aware. In everyday life, one focuses one's attention either on one's inner world or on the external world around them, often moving between the two states in succession.

Trance encounters each one of us every day, not only in the treatment room. It is a state of waking hypnosis that we experience everywhere: at work, while driving, during a meal, while swimming for long periods in the sea or a pool, in conversations with friends, on dates, and even at nightclubs.

Sometimes it is difficult to distinguish between trance and a natural, ordinary state of relaxation and calm. Many people may be in a trance state without even realizing it. Who among you, for example, hasn't been so absorbed in a movie or a contest that you disconnected from the world around you? Who among you hasn't become engrossed in a fascinating and enjoyable conversation with someone—for hours at times—seeing nothing but animated faces and losing track of time? Who among you hasn't sat in a quiet, beautiful, and romantic place while your thoughts drifted far away?

Everyone is very familiar with trance, as it is a state into which one regularly sinks in daily life. Yet one exits it, only to immediately return to it again. When traveling on a long journey, one is in a trance during many parts of the trip, drifting into daydreams.

Since trance is a rich and active state—and even allows for a connection with the unconscious to effect change—reaching and achieving it constitutes a fundamental element and a first step in transmitting positive therapeutic messages and in working toward the therapeutic goal for which the patient sought treatment.

The process of creating trance is extremely important, since one will not reach the subconscious without it. The hypnotist diverts the attention of the conscious mind and engages it so that it can penetrate the brain, the unconscious, or the inner mind.

Chapter 5

Erickson's Language and Its Role in Hypnosis

Milton Erickson understood the importance of language for a person and its impact on them. He possessed an extraordinary ability to induce anyone into a state of trance by using linguistic skills that activate the conscious, logical, and analytical parts—which are considered the guardians of the patient's unconscious—and to bring them into a state of complete hypnosis, and thereafter to transmit an emotion, thought, or suggestion at the subconscious level that would help them deal with the situation from which they wish to extricate themselves or to treat.

Types of linguistic skills

- **Positive assumptions:** This skill is based on attributing a positive meaning to a statement in relation to the listener. For example, someone might say to you, "Keep enjoying reading these words." The implied assumption here is that you were already enjoying them, and therefore, the feeling of enjoyment will continue.

- **Implanting thoughts:** This skill is based on transmitting subconscious thoughts by suggesting that the other person's thoughts can be read. For example, a manager might say to an employee, "I know that you will do everything you can to improve your work." In doing so, the manager implants the idea of taking action to enhance performance in the employee's subconscious. Another example: someone tells a friend, "I know you feel comfortable in this place." If they indeed feel comfortable, they will likely be surprised that their friend knows it; and if they do not feel at ease, their friend's words will reinforce their sense of comfort. Or statements such as, "I know I can rely on you," "I'm sure you make a point of preparing your lessons on your own." Or instead of replying "You're welcome" or "My pleasure" to thanks, one might say, "In my place, you would do the same," thereby implanting a thought and inviting future action while "preparing" the person for eventual reciprocation. All these are examples of sentences and expressions that imply that someone might be able to read another's thoughts, thus causing them to believe and strengthen those thoughts.

- **Fostering possibility and desire rather than necessity:** Using this skill, the desire is gently guided in such a way that the person comes to perceive that the wish originates from within themselves. For example, you might say to a friend, "You surely want to accompany me to...", or you might tell your child, "I see that you want to succeed," "I see that you want to do this or that," "I see that you want to tackle the problem," "I see that you want to speak in front of the class freely, fluidly, and in a confident voice," and so on.

- **The simple association:** Through this skill, it is possible to link two problems or two ideas by using the conjunction "and". This connection is between a tangible fact and an accompanying emotion, for example: "You are reading my words right now, and you are enjoying it," or "You begin to zone out when you watch television."

- **The implied association:** Through this skill, we connect a real situation with the message or emotion we wish to convey, in order to encourage the listener to further sink into the state they are in. For instance, the statements: "While you are sitting, you feel relaxed," "In the midst of thinking, the solution will reveal itself to you," "The more you continue to read the article, the more you will understand the lesson,"

"While you watch the sun vanish into the sea, you feel tranquility," "The more the sun sets, the more you sink (or enter) into a wonderful feeling of confidence and serenity."

- **Quotations:** With this skill, one can influence the subconscious of the listener by conveying information that one does not want to attribute directly to oneself, and therefore, it is stated as if coming from someone else. One can also speak on behalf of a third party to pass along information to someone, a piece of information that is important to them and in their best interest.

  This is done so that the information does not come directly from you, as it might evoke resistance and rejection from your interlocutor, making it difficult for them to accept. For example, we say: "My friends tell me I look great when I speak in front of everyone," "These things don't really matter, but my brother insisted on saying them," "I'm not sure that this will appeal to you, but research shows that anger causes many serious illnesses," "My friend told me that hypnosis helped him immensely overcome his fear of exams." We do not limit the use of these linguistic skills exclusively to the treatment room and hypnosis. Certainly, they can also be applied in our daily communications with others, in the educational process, and relationships between parents and their children.

- **Double bind and choosing one of two:** In this skill, I will elaborate at length, given its importance in the educational process, and not only there. By using this skill, a person receives two or more contradictory messages, with one message negating the other. A situation is created in which a successful response to one message results in a failed response to the other, or vice versa. This is an effective way to market or convey an idea when the listener shows resistance.
  Examples: "I wonder if you want to go swimming or visit the zoo." In this sentence, the two possible alternatives are subconsciously defined, leaving the person with no option but to choose one of them. Does one say to a young child who is beginning to show a tendency toward independence: "Do you want to wear the white shirt or the blue one?" or "Do you want a sandwich with cheese or with jelly?" or "Do you want to study before lunch or after it?" All these examples present the child with two alternatives (there can even be three) that his mother has predetermined for him. This skill is very important in education, as it gives the child the opportunity to decide on their own—thereby reinforcing and encouraging the development of their sense of independence and taking

> responsibility for their decision within the framework set by their parents and in accordance with the norms, values, and educational boundaries they believe in.

Of course, it is possible to use this double bind in every stage of life and every situation in daily life, in society, and at school. "Sure, you can spend the night out, but tell me what time you'll be back—at ten or eleven?" (i.e., I agree that you may go out at night, but I will set the latest time by which you must be home), or "Which subject would you prefer to start studying — mathematics or physics?" (i.e., you will choose which subject to begin with, but there is no dispute about the necessity of studying), and so on.

In this context, I recall that a friend of my little daughter wanted to spend the night at her place. Since her father did not agree to his daughter sleeping outside the home — and she was aware of this — she asked me how she could persuade him. She called him on the phone and said, "Dad, I'm staying over tonight at Saosan's. What time is it convenient for you to come and pick me up in the morning? At nine or ten?" For her father, that "scheme" caught him completely off guard, leaving him with no alternative. The issue was not so much her spending the night out as it was the time in the morning when he would come to pick her up. Of course, he hurried to reply, and she laughed and jumped for joy as she put down the phone receiver.

In order to enter hypnosis, it is possible to present two alternatives, especially to those who show resistance or difficulty in entering it: "You can enter hypnosis quickly or slowly" or "with your eyes closed or open"... There is no doubt that the person is about to enter hypnosis; the only question is how, and that is what he decides based on the alternatives set by the therapist.

This method is often used in telephone marketing. The phone rings, and on the other end, the voice of the marketer is heard:

"Hello, hi, is there anyone with me?"

"Yes."

"How are you, sir? Congratulations, you've won a gift from Company X. We would like to send it to you. Tell me, please, what kind of credit card do you have—Visa or MasterCard?"

Usually, an immediate answer is given regarding the type of credit card, since the marketer has limited the options. And from there, things begin to roll...

CHAPTER 6

HYPNOSIS AND PAIN MANAGEMENT

The role of pain is to serve as a warning against some form of damage or a physical problem that has not yet been detected. When a person feels pain, it is a sign that there is an issue requiring treatment. The body has its own self-healing mechanisms for these situations, as it secretes chemical substances called opioids to reduce pain. In pharmacies, many medications perform this very function.

Approaching the treatment of chronic pain through hypnosis involves several aspects, and one must consider the components of the patient's personality—their traits, needs, and motives.

It can be said that, in a sense, pain represents a loss of control, since the person feels incapable of controlling their body. Hypnosis helps the patient strengthen control over both their body and the pain. Moreover, hypnosis opens up horizons to different ways and possibilities to treat pain, to cope with it, and to change one's attitude toward it. However, before any intervention to reduce pain using hypnosis, essential medical examinations must be conducted to determine the underlying causes of the pain in the first place. If organic causes for the pain are ruled out, hypnosis can play a central role in the patient's management of the pain. But even in cases where organic causes are found, hypnosis can help accelerate and optimize conventional treatment.

The brain releases a chemical substance called endorphins. This substance, which is similar to morphine yet devoid of addictive side effects, is responsible for diminishing pain. Its capability to eliminate pain even surpasses that of morphine, and it constitutes an important part of the brain's defense mechanisms against stress, anxiety, and agitation. The secretion of this substance profoundly affects emotions and behavior, which explains the feeling of calm experienced by a person under hypnosis, as its release increases during the process. It also explains why individuals whose brains secrete larger amounts of endorphins can bear pain better than those whose brains resist the secretion of this substance.

The type of strategy used to control pain is determined largely by the personality of the hypnotized subject and their willingness to be hypnotized, as well as by the personality of the hypnotist and their ability to select the appropriate method of hypnosis. Hypnosis is also employed in the treatment of individuals suffering from chronic back pain, and to ease uterine contractions during labor—especially in its early stages—without resorting to painkillers or anesthetic substances. In the second stage of labor, only mild painkillers are used according to the condition of the mother and the degree of her trust in suggestion.

One of the reasons that convinces a woman to agree to

hypnosis during labor is the knowledge that she will remain aware of what is happening and be an active participant in the birth, especially since most mothers fear the effects of anesthetic agents on the newborn. Moreover, women have become more aware of methods for controlling labor contractions and of using self-suggestion through rhythmic, regular, deep breathing that diverts the mother's attention away from the pain and directs her thoughts toward her breathing and counting. This causes the sensation of pain to vanish and shortens the interval between each stage of labor, since the onset of each contraction serves as a signal for her to achieve a deep hypnotic relaxation, with the end of each contraction leading her out of that state.

Chapter 7

Methods of Treating Pain Through Hypnosis

There are several ways to treat pain using hypnosis. For example, one can remove the pain from the body or separate it from the body and perceive it as an independent entity that is not connected to the human form. This can also be achieved by anesthetizing another area of the body—for instance, the palm—and then prompting the patient, through suggestion, to transfer the numbness to the area of pain and gradually numb it.

In hypnosis, one can also work with metaphors or images that the patient attributes to the pain.

The Metaphor

The metaphor is a symbolic tool of communication, a kind of painting in language that helps unveil hidden psychological processes. It transforms anxiety from an illogical language into images that one can more easily contend with without having to seek permission from reason. It then allows the story to be reformulated.

Since what we tell ourselves after an event is what affects us—not the event itself—the patient can, through metaphor, reconstruct the experience in a new way or retell the story differently.

Often, we use metaphors in our daily conversations when trying to explain something. For instance, we say "I love you to the skies" to describe a positive emotion of immense love for a dear person, or "I'm flying with happiness" to describe joy. Yet we also say "knives are slicing my stomach into pieces" to portray a negative sensation of stomach pain, or "hammers are pounding in my head" to describe a headache, "a large stone is resting on my heart" to depict a state of pressure or difficulty breathing, or "fire is bursting from my eyes" to express anger, irritability, or a sharp rise in body temperature.

One can also use the metaphor as an effective therapeutic tool, for by employing the description provided by the patient, it becomes possible to influence the psychological and neuropsychological processes he is undergoing, and through them affect his subconscious. This process furnishes tools to help the person overcome their problem.

According to Erickson, the psychosomatic symptoms and complaints themselves are a metaphor expressing a change that has occurred in a person's life. Thus, communication through metaphor can help the individual better define the course of that change.

In a hypnotic state, the metaphor wields great power and has a profound impact on the patient's condition, contributing significantly to shortening the treatment period. Therapy using metaphor is conducted by appealing to the subconscious world, which influences the conscious mind and other psychological processes directly and effortlessly, such as defense mechanisms and resistances that may arise during conventional psychotherapy. And that is exactly what gives it its power. Moreover, studies in the field of the nervous system indicate that the metaphor activates the right side of the brain, processing information in a synchronized, non-logical manner through images, symbols, and hints. In contrast, the language of anxiety, used by those complaining of pain, activates the left side of the brain, which processes information in a linear, systematic, logical, decisive, and goal-oriented fashion.

Two of the stories in this book deal with treatment using metaphor, and here I will also present a few brief examples.

It is enough for a person who feels "knives" in his stomach to close his eyes and imagine these "knives," to count them, to describe their brightness, their color, the depth of their penetration into his stomach, and so on, and then to precisely imagine how these "knives" are removed from his stomach, and the ways in which he uses to extract them. This process must be carried out slowly, quietly, and gradually.

During one of the workshops in which we practiced hypnosis, I was assigned the task of treating a colleague who was suffering from severe shoulder pain. Once he entered a trance state, I asked him to describe this pain to me. He told me that the pain was like a fire originating in his shoulder, spreading to the upper part of his back and his neck. When I asked him what was needed to extinguish the fire, he replied,

"Only a small super-tanker can put it out" (this was just a few days after the fires had spread over Mt. Carmel — a situation that forced the authorities to seek help from abroad, and among other things, a huge American super-tanker plane was dispatched, receiving extensive media coverage). All that was required of both him and me, while he was in a hypnotic state, was to summon a small super-tanker plane and activate it so that it could spray the powerful substance specially brought to extinguish the fire that had spread over his shoulder, the upper part of his back, and his neck. "Here comes the super-tanker plane from afar, approaching quietly, and it looks larger and larger as it draws near... it draws nearer and nearer... and here it is, right above the target... here it is above your shoulder, the upper part of your back, and your neck... it sprays a special, refreshing substance that was brought solely to extinguish the fire spreading over your back... your shoulder... your neck... Here is the substance that not only puts out the fire, but also energizes the body as it touches it... the fire begins to subside slowly... the plane sprays the remaining reserve of the special substance it carries... a substance descending from the air and dispersing within you, with droplets reaching your shoulder, your back... your neck... throughout your entire body... the fire diminishes more and more, and the body feels increasingly alert and refreshed... the plane completes its task... gradually moves away... it soars in the air and recedes further and further... as it retreats and diminishes, the feeling of calm and well-being in your body grows stronger... a pleasant, refreshing sensation gradually spreads through your body..."

Thus, for two or three rounds, the plane sprayed the

refreshing substance until the fire was finally extinguished and the pain disappeared.

Another case: a woman in her thirties suffered from being underweight. She weighed less than forty kilograms, and all her attempts to gain weight amounted to nothing. Comprehensive general medical examinations showed that she was healthy and ruled out any medical reason for her underweight condition. The nutritional supplements, various vitamins she took, and her special dietary practices did not help, and her weight did not increase. Her dream was to reach a weight of forty-six kilograms.

At the beginning of the first therapy session, I asked her why the body (any body, not specifically hers) was unable to gain weight. I requested that she describe the reason to me using some image or metaphor, and she said:

"My stomach is small, very small. It has no room for an amount of food sufficient to cause weight gain. It's like a small child's stomach."

During the hypnosis, and after she entered a state of deep trance, I said to her:

"...when you're in this state, you surely understand how important love, warmth, and compassion are—qualities that are bestowed upon a child so that he may grow and develop... Studies have proven that emotional warmth, which includes touch, caress, and hugs, is essential for building the nervous system and the brain..."

The hugs, love, and warmth are central elements and basic conditions for a child to grow and develop... to grow and develop... The more the father and the mother hug their child and express their love for them, the better they will develop and they will grow up healthier... Hugs, warmth, and love are the most important foundations for every living creature, whether it be a child, an animal, or even a plant... They say that when a person hugs a plant and transfers energy to it from his hands, it accelerates its growth and blossoming... Since this affects all of these, perhaps you will be surprised to learn that the warmth you supply to your stomach will enlarge it... cause it to grow, expand, and flourish... just as with a small child, so is your stomach, which resembles a small child's stomach... If you speak to it, lay your hands upon it, close your eyes, and bestow upon it love and warmth, it will open up and expand... develop and feel secure... and grow... just as happens with children... so too will your stomach—like that of a small child—grow. Both are small, and both grow and develop thanks to love, warmth, caresses, and hugs... Love brings growth, warmth evokes a sense of security, and a hug leads to expansion and growth... of the stomach, of the child, of plants, of the little animals nestled in the arms of their mothers in search of milk, warmth, and security..."

We all use metaphors for description, and we can use them to treat pain, fear, or various states of anxiety.

During hypnosis, the hammers pounding in one's head cease, the knives cutting into the stomach are withdrawn, and the stone weighing upon the heart or back is removed.

I treated a boy who suffered from alopecia, a condition that causes hair loss in certain areas of the head and the formation of bald patches.

Among the methods I employed during the hypnotherapeutic treatment of the boy were metaphor and imagery.

After we together recalled how the immune system functions in the body and how white blood cells attack the microbes and other foreign invaders that infiltrate the body, I induced him into a state of hypnosis and engaged him in the following conversation:

"Focus on the skin of your head and tell me what you see there."

"I see armies arrayed... all carrying similar weapons... the same uniform and the same color... all standing in a single line, ready to defend and repel any attack."

"Good, are these armies spread throughout all areas of your head?"

"Not at all..."

"Describe to me... what is happening..."

"There are certain areas where I see no armies... I see several wounded soldiers lying on the ground... vast quantities of microbes devouring everything in their path... they have cut down everything that appeared before them..."

"So what do we do now? There are strong armies... armed... arrayed... preparing to defend... and nearby, in certain areas, there is an assault by microbes that devour everything they encounter..."

"I will ask for help and direct some of the armies to those areas..."

"You can deploy all the armies needed to those areas. You know that attack is also important for defense... it is essential to protect the remaining healthy areas..."

By means of hypnosis and according to my instructions, the boy began directing the necessary number of soldiers to the areas described as "the eaten, the conquered, the burnt, the shortened, the bald." A fierce battle ensued, resulting in many soldier casualties, but in the process, all the microbes were neutralized. The boy smiled as he described how the microbes cried out while falling, and how the soldiers pursued while the microbes fled for their lives. Two sessions of intense combat and fierce warfare concluded with the eradication of all the microbes, followed by a thorough search and comprehensive cleansing of every area to ensure that no external enemy remained in the head.

After two weeks of practicing self-hypnosis at home, hair was already beginning to grow in the bald areas.

Hypnosis has enjoyed great success in improving behaviors and in transforming many bad habits, in treating obesity caused by overeating, and in managing insomnia through deep relaxation training and a quiet, peaceful dive into a restful night's sleep. Self-hypnosis is the pathway to a regular night's sleep—it is the threshold of sleep, guiding the mind from "Beta" to "Alpha", then to "Theta" and finally to Delta, which is sleep.

Hypnosis is also one of the forms of mental training, and thus it has the potential to enhance athletic abilities; indeed, it can help athletes reach a state of relaxation during competition as well as assist them in controlling feelings of anxiety and managing exertion. It further helps athletes cope with personal challenges that could negatively affect their performance. Hypnosis also helps to focus bodily awareness, heighten its level, and ease the intensity of pain.

Many coaches have successfully employed hypnosis as a means to encourage their players to believe in and visualize their victories in competitions, thereby alleviating the anxiety and tension they had experienced beforehand. Research shows that training through visualization activates the same areas in the brain as physical training, and indeed, imagery constitutes "mental training" that improves performance.[4] This has made hypnosis a successful method and a tool that helps secure victory in various kinds of sports. The reason is that all physical activities are essentially mental ones. Moreover, an athlete's performance will be better if they can understand their goal, believe in their ability to achieve it, and visualize it, since the body does everything that is required of it, as long as the request is reasonable.

The athlete brings his personality to the competition, and in his eyes, it is not only the defeat of the opponent that counts as victory, but also his own inner sense of triumph. When a player practices self-hypnosis, he enters a state of complete focus that creates a channel of communication between the brain and the body's movements, thus achieving a high level of skill and self-confidence throughout the competition.

Hypnosis contributes to stimulating the learning process in students by teaching them ways to harness the intellectual potential inherent in them, and later, also their creativity. It is used to overcome obstacles that impede progress, such as various states of fear and feelings of low self-confidence. Before exams, students may feel a fear of failure, which causes some of them to experience complete mental blankness, especially on the eve of or during the exam. Focused attention aids in assimilating, altering, and retrieving information. Hypnosis succeeds in strengthening the sense of calm and concentration, thereby contributing to an improved learning process. This is also true in language learning, as it helps a person recall a language they knew perfectly in their youth but later forgot, thus helping to recover lost information and bring it back to life—a difference that clearly distinguishes success from failure in any educational endeavor.

Hypnosis is used to help break harmful habits, such as smoking and drinking alcoholic beverages, and to treat organic diseases like high blood pressure, especially in women; it alleviates rheumatic pain, joint pain, toothaches, menstrual cramps, labor pains, and ulcers. It helps to bear the excruciating pain of burns and to prevent migraines. Hypnosis has been successfully applied in the treatment of conditions such as nocturnal anxiety, involuntary nocturnal enuresis, loss of appetite, and excessive appetite. It also yields positive results in several disorders—for example, speech delays, stuttering, the restoration of the voice after its loss, nail-biting, and more.

Part Two

Stories from the Hypnosis Treatment Clinic

Chapter 8

The Lady

Dealing with Loss

She had not yet been born when her mother was diagnosed with "that disease whose name must not be mentioned"–cancer.

In fact, her mother had not yet married when she was diagnosed with "that disease."

Her mother was still a child when the disease attacked her, and no one expected her to recover.

They said she would die before reaching adulthood, but she continued to live and achieved maturity.

They said she would never be able to have children, but she married and bore children.

They said she would die and leave her young children orphaned—as if she were the one who gives life, causes death and orphans children—but she was blessed with grandchildren.

They said she wouldn't reach the age of forty, yet she celebrated her eighty-third birthday.

And then she died.

She is “The Lady”.

Her mother was hospitalized for six days, during which her spirit did not falter and her smile never left her lips.

Miriam spent six days by her mother’s side in the hospital. The mother knew that, in the end, she would die, and the daughter did not doubt it. Yet the close bond between them—the mutual, symbiotic connection—prevented them from fully comprehending this, or rather, from coming to terms with her impending death. The heart was stronger than the mind, and out of their love and devotion to each other, they fought for her to live on forever.

Miriam couldn’t quite grasp what happened at the moment her mother opened her eyes and looked at her for a few seconds with a strange, unfamiliar gaze, then sighed deeply and fell asleep.

In her gaze, there was a sorrow intermingled with a silent message, and she bid farewell.

A sharp beeping sound emanated from the screen hanging above her head, in the center of which a steady, horizontal red line was visible. Eventually, the sea calmed, and the stormy waves rising and falling in harmony subsided — albeit with a force and speed exceeding one hundred and twenty wave pulses per minute.

"Maybe she has reached her destination and stopped to rest," she whispered to herself.

She heard no response. A strange silence pervaded the room. She saw the nurses and doctors attending to her mother, their mouths agape as they conversed among themselves, but she heard nothing. Suddenly, she couldn't tell whether it was she who had given up her own ghost, or whether it was her mother's soul that had taken flight.

She floated in the air, watching, observing, following every movement, yet she heard nothing and was unable to touch anything or communicate with anyone. She opened her mouth to scream, but no sound emerged. No one noticed her. Everyone was busy with a complete body from which nothing was lacking—applying a defibrillator to the chest once, twice, three times... She realized that something had happened, that her mother had died, yet she did not understand what this death truly meant. Is this how people die?

It was the first time she had seen someone die, and she couldn't process it. The body lying before her was intact. There was no change in her mother. Admittedly, her body was somewhat cold, and her once-beautiful skin had yellowed, but that is normal in a state of immobility, she tried to convince herself. Her head, her hair, her eyes... yes, her eyes were closed, yet they were in place, as were her mouth, her hands, her feet. In short, everything about her, more or less.

What does "died" mean? Does the roaring of the storm on the screen signify death? Must life, in all its aspects, be bustling and noisy to prove that she is alive and breathing?

Does silence mean death?

Countless questions raced through her mind — questions that had long preoccupied her — and she found no answers to any of them.

All she knew was that "The Lady" had parted from life at that very moment.

It was in February, exactly eight months ago.

Miriam wore her finest clothes to the funeral — a black dress embroidered with various floral patterns in white and red, black shoes with medium heels, and a brown, spring scarf that covered her black hair, from which a few white strands had emerged.

Two months had passed since she had last dyed her hair, and it was time for her to visit the hairdresser; however, that very day she was tending to her mother on her hospital bed and didn't even dare to think about it. The idea didn't seem proper to her, and perhaps she feared pangs of conscience. How could she leave her mother, who was fighting for her life, to go to the hairdresser and spend hours dyeing her hair to appear younger? And perhaps, while sitting in the hairdresser's chair on that black leather seat, perusing magazines or engaging in conversation with other clients, her mother's soul might depart? How would she be remembered in the future? What will she say when asked where she was when...?

Will you answer: "When my mother died, I was at the hairdresser's"?

Oh, to dream such horrors!

"When my mother died, I was by her side, holding her hand!"

That is what she would wish to take pride in—first and foremost in herself—when she recalls the moment of parting from her mother.

The next day, she smiled at herself and others, thereby carrying out her mother's last wishes, and she calmly accepted the presence of the mourners and those who wept sincere, quiet tears. As if grief had been transformed into a dark joy, she requested that visitors respect the repose and said that anyone who wished to cry should do so quietly, without shouting, without eulogies, without hair-pulling, and without feigned sorrow.

Astonished glances were cast her way from the people around her. Some described her as crazy, while others claimed she was brazen and shameless.

Miriam holds a master's degree in social work and is working on her doctorate, determined to follow in her mother's footsteps and be just like her.

She is married and has one child. Despite the pressures from those around her — those who cared for her well-being but abandoned her in times of crisis— she remained steadfast in her decision to have only one child.

I do not know much about her husband. To be fair and precise, I know nothing about him. He was never mentioned in my conversations with her, and I do not know what his occupation is, what his level of education is, how old he is... All I know is that his name is Roni.

It appears that he was intermittently present in her life. I thought there was no need to delve into these details during the initial stage of treatment; rather, I understood that there was an urgent need to address directly the burning issue for which she had come to me. Therefore, I decided to postpone the discussion about her relationship with her husband and the reason for his absence to a later time, should the need arise and if Miriam agreed.

If we go back a little, we find that when Miriam turned fifteen, she realized that her mother still existed "for she was not dead, not yet." Every moment could have been fateful, and every day could have been her last. Yet the sun continued to shine on both of them every morning, and the smile kept spreading across their faces every time they met.

It was a smile that both understood and meant so much to them, even though they never proclaimed it publicly, not even once.

It was the smile of victory over death.

Both felt life in every single minute, and although it was never stated explicitly, neither of them took for granted that tomorrow would come, especially for "The Lady," whom the doctors had estimated would live at most until the age of forty.

Every moment after forty was a gift to them.

Every meeting between them felt like the first after a long absence, and every farewell seemed like the final one.

Thus passed forty-three years, thousands of meetings, and thousands of gifts.

Finally, "The Lady" died, as Miriam used to call her mother.

And she was left alone.

Despite those around her, "those who cared for her well-being, yet abandoned her in times of distress."

When I listen to Miriam's story, I sink into my memory.

I was about six or seven years old when thoughts and fears about my mother's death began to appear.

There were ten of us at home—brothers and sisters—and a mother who did everything in her power so that we would live and continue to breathe, and, no less importantly, that we would breathe with dignity.

She was widowed in her thirties, young and beautiful. She never remarried and dedicated the remainder of her life —about fifty years—to children who all became parents, and some even became grandparents. Mom always reminded us of our late father's advice, his good qualities, and the "set" plan for each one of us, and she worked hard to see those plans come to fruition.

And she succeeded!

It was by no means an easy burden for a widow, facing the views and attitudes of a traditional society, providing for a large family, immersed in worries and debts, and all the while upholding immense self-respect.

I was one of the younger siblings, and naturally, my older siblings had already experienced the challenges of growing up. Adolescence is never easy, and it certainly wasn't for my mother, who did not know how to read or write or how to seek psychological guidance, yet she followed the dictates of her heart and her love for us.

In the moments when she felt that she could no longer bear the burden of responsibility for raising her ten children at home, she would cry, alone... And I was afraid that she wouldn't hold on, that she would abandon us and vanish, yet she never let a moment pass without being completely with us, with all of us.

No holiday passed without the scent of date-filled cookies permeating the house.

No holiday passed without thoughts and fears seeping into my very being. I would watch my mother as she prepared the cookies, quietly crying, for I was convinced that by the next holiday, she would no longer bake them, because she would die.

Yet she remained with us until I turned fifty, and she was eighty.

She was a gift to me for almost forty-five years.

Yet the child within me remained seven.

Miriam was at the institution, holding a therapeutic session with the parents of a child in need of special care. Recently, the parents had received a notice from the Child Development Unit that their three-year-old son suffered from a severe, general developmental intellectual disability. Therefore, he was referred, via the bureau, to a rehabilitative treatment facility specializing in this field.

It was her third meeting with the parents and the first with the child himself, who lay in his stroller—a neglected child whose body did not match his age, with tanned skin and large eyes. Miriam gazed into his sparkling eyes and saw light and life; she looked into his mother's eyes and saw fear and sorrow; she looked into his father's eyes and all she saw was silence and helplessness.

"What will become of this child when he grows up? How will he live his life? Will he die?"

"The one and only God, in his hands everything lies, woman," said the man to his wife as they raised their hands to the sky, his hands clutching a rosary of ninety-nine beads.

Indeed, that is so... the woman whispered to herself, he will live with dignity, marry and have children, and they will grow up to love him—she thought. That was her hope.

Miriam tried to exude optimism in the eyes of her mother, aware that her mother might die of grief if she allowed herself to imagine the fate awaiting her son in a society that shows insufficient understanding for those with special needs and sometimes even regards them as objects of ridicule and exclusion.

Although society's attitude toward individuals with special needs is not as it once was, and despite the positive shift that has taken place, the situation remains dismal—even very dismal—for several population groups, especially among the rural population.

This mother, a simple woman with basic education and a warm, loving heart, knew nothing of the subject. She only knew the story of that girl whose parents had confined her in a room within the house for years. Perhaps they did it out of love, or to protect her, or to avoid "disgrace." It was many years before — twenty years or more.

"That's all I know about disabled children," she told Miriam. "The image of that girl never leaves me, and sometimes that poor soul appears in my dreams. May God heal them all, the poor souls..."

However, that mother also knew that such forced confinement achieved none of its intended aims. For the "disgrace" was known to all, and the parents' destructive love could neither help her nor protect her from an early death. And indeed, she died young, at the onset of her youth. The mother recalled that it was the smallest funeral procession she had ever seen. The girl's father carried his daughter's body, wrapped in white, in his arms instead of a coffin. A few relatives and friends — no more than two handfuls — joined him.

Miriam's cell phone rang, and her mother's number appeared on the screen. Her pulse froze, for her mother never disturbed her during work except for something essential. She excused herself to her clients and answered. From the other end came the voice of her little brother. Her heart pounded rapidly, and she felt that what he feared most was materializing before her eyes.

"Salim, what about Mom? Why are you speaking on her phone? Hand her over to me."

"Miriam, calm down. She's in the hospital. Her condition is stable. Don't be afraid. They have just taken her into the operating room."

What a difficult moment this is! My mother is being taken into the operating room while I am here at work, she thought, setting a hard challenge for herself: I must now choose between my mother and the mother before me.

No... how overwhelming the fear, and how immense the shared sorrow between me and this mother!

My mother never feared death; on the contrary, she awaited it, yet it refused to come.

"It seems that death is afraid of those who are unafraid of it... afraid of those who are unafraid of it..." she murmured again.

Fortunately, she had managed to build a good rapport and earn the family's trust, which allowed her to apologize and rush to the hospital, to her mother, a mother who did not fear death.

Miriam found her in the intensive care unit, still under the effects of anesthesia and connected to a mechanical ventilator.

She sat beside her and held her hand.

"Don't go, Mom, please... please, don't leave me alone. I have no one but you."

She said that, but immediately understood that by doing

so, she was burdening her mother, especially since she knew it was beyond her control.

"God, what shall I say? What is happening to me? Is my mother the one who will decide? If so, there is no doubt she will choose to come back to us... to me."

Finally, she decided to remain silent and pray quietly, and between prayer and hope she whispered to her mother —whom she loved so dearly—that she loved her.

In those moments, she felt an intense need for her mother's support and longed to climb into bed and lie in her embrace, perhaps for the last time. She felt a powerful urge to cry and wail out loud, yet she needed a hand to caress her back as she wept. Where is that hand now?

Miriam had never received from anyone the sense of security that her mother had provided her. In fact, those around her did not even notice her presence. She created, acted, struggled, and accomplished what "the lady" had taught her, but the more she stood out and excelled, the more her transparency emerged, and her radiance diminished in the eyes of those "who cared about her well-being."

How absurd and surreal this feeling is. She seeks comfort and support from her mother — who lies on a deathbed — so that she can cope with her mother's imminent passing.

How strange this feeling is, and how hard it is to understand. Yet one whose hand is ablaze feels nothing but pain, and one who suffers clings to anything to hold on to.

At that moment, the "lady" reacted. She quietly pressed her daughter's finger that lay in her hand, opened her eyes for a moment, looked directly into her daughter's eyes, and then went back to sleep.

Miriam smiled, and tearful sorrows mixed with joy streamed from her eyes.

In the days that followed, Miriam did not leave her mother's bedside, day or night. She realized that the remaining moments of her mother's life were few, dependent on the oxygen tubes. All she now desired, and for the final time, was a grasp—even a small, frail one—of her mother's finger and one last brief look into her eyes. She wanted no words, and even relinquished the idea of a hug or a caress on her back, for it was clear that all of those were impossible.

Just one last glance and a gentle touch. Is that too much to ask?

"It's all over, Miriam, that's it. Our mother is dead. The 'lady' has departed."

She heard the voice drawing near and felt a hand holding her, gently pulling her away from the bed.

My mother lay in the hospital for three days after suffering a stroke caused by a severe brain hemorrhage, which made her lose consciousness and control over her body.

For three days, I wondered if I could let my mother go.

My mother's wish was to live without being a burden on anyone and to die with the dignity and pride she had maintained all her life. Even on her final day, before the stroke visited her, she did not give in and continued to stand on her own, despite the many illnesses she suffered. Under no circumstances did she agree to return to her home, paralyzed and dependent on the help of others.

I knew that she would rather die than be subjected to the pity of others.

Moreover, she feared suffering and becoming a victim of mistreatment by those who might assist her, having seen and heard on television how the elderly and helpless are treated in private homes, nursing homes, and care institutions around the country.

I decided to let her go...

As if the matter were solely in my hands.

I decided, this time, to let her go with love, for my heart was certain that she had fulfilled her mission and carried out her maternal duty in the best possible way.

But I did not succeed.

I did not cry when my mother died, either, like Miriam. I do not know where I drew the strength from. For three days, I greeted the consolers with a smile and endeavored to maintain an outward appearance that would have pleased "the lady," my lady, and who would undoubtedly have been very proud of me.

Every morning, Miriam plucked two roses or another plant from her home garden and went to visit her mother's grave in the family cemetery at the center of the village. She placed the flowers in the vase she had set on the grave and replaced the ones she had brought previously. In a plot of land beside the grave, she had planted a few sage saplings whose fragrance would rise to her nostrils every time she entered her mother's house.

Miriam sat for several minutes at the edge of the grave, built of white stone, and engaged in a quiet conversation with nothing but her body. She kissed the grave in place of a head and feet and recited the "Alfatecha"[5], then continued on her way to the institution where she worked.

No one knew what Miriam was thinking, what she was saying, or what her true feelings were.

But I know, even though Miriam never told me this. She felt a deep loneliness, and in the depths of her heart, she hoped to be engulfed by that place, if she could not somehow extract her mother from it.

She would return to her mother's house, where she had lived with security and warmth for most of her life, to search for her mother's scent, for a trace of her hair among the white tufts on her head, or for something to hold to her chest—to embrace and be embraced in return.

Everything in the house remained just as it was—the mother's bed, the living room, the wardrobe... but the medicine cabinet that had accompanied her mother through her "extra" years had vanished. Miriam was very angry with the women who hurried to clean the house immediately after the burial. If only she could, she would rearrange the house and leave it just as it had been when "the lady" left it for the last time. At least then she would find consolation in realizing that she was incapable of restoring her own body.

She would sit on the bed, running her hand over the mattress, the pillow, and the iron frame, perhaps encountering fingerprints and marks that no cleaning hand had erased. Thus, she would sit for an hour or more, closing her eyes, engaging her sense of smell, and following remnants here and there. Vivid, distant images would arise before her eyes as she reconstructed memories and moments that filled her with love, sorrow, and strength. Afterwards, she would go to her work to breathe life into those in need.

For eight months, she followed this path.

"She lives within me," she said.

"You hold her inside you," I said, reproaching my patient —or perhaps projecting it onto her.

She did not respond. Her face suddenly reddened from the shock, the blow she had sustained, or perhaps it was the brazenness of the therapist. How dare he say what he did?

Or perhaps it was because she was confronted with a truth that no one had seen or voiced.

"She is dead," I tried to explain to her, "but you still haven't let her go; you still hold her within you with love, and you struggle to revive her again and restore her to the way she once was."

"She's not dead. She lives within me."

"Her memory—that is what lives within you."

I realized that there was a need to deal with death and process the loss. It was clear to me that she was in a phase of denial, unable to accept her mother's cruel death—a stage in which she felt isolated and helpless, and no one could fill the role of "the lady" and take her place in her life. No one could provide her with the warmth she had suddenly lost, even though she knew that her mother had lived for many years as a "gift" and had long been destined to die, not just eight months ago. She yearned for that maternal compassion, that love, that sense of security she had once felt deep within every pore of her body and in the depths of her soul. She sought that feeling as if it were an all-consuming obsession in one place—a grave from which nothing could ever emerge except a few sage saplings. Perhaps she sanctified the scent that rose from her mother's grave through those saplings, but she longed for a body that would embrace her; she craved genuine warmth and a hand to caress her hair and face, her soul and her heart.

Where will you get all of that?

Many months passed during which she went to search for them in the cemetery, but all in vain.

The people living near the cemetery began to follow her and cast questioning glances her way. Generally, the relatives of the deceased visit the cemetery once a week, usually on Fridays. In the initial period—during the first month or the first two or three months—some come once or twice a week, or at most three times a week. But not for eight months! This is the visiting frequency familiar to them and, in their experience, the reasonable period for visits, without any need for scientific research on the subject. By the way, they even knew the visiting hours and could predict the visitors' behavior from the moment they entered the cemetery until they left. They noticed a similarity in the way many of the visitors behaved upon entering the place. Everyone basically stands in the same spot, opens their hands in front of their face, and recites the Al-Fatiha or some prayer; then they wipe their faces with their hands and enter. Upon leaving, they repeat the same ritual. Everyone does so, regardless of their degree of faith in God, their strict observance of religious commandments, their political affiliation, their level of knowledge and education, and even their gender. They say that men do not cry. Whoever truly believes that should come to the cemetery, hide behind one of the tombs or behind the curtains of one of the nearby houses—if they have any connection with the neighbors—and watch the visitors. Then they will see men quietly shedding tears. It goes without saying that they do cry; the men here cry. Death is hard on everyone and does not discriminate among people. Grief strikes everyone without exception.

And everyone cries.

However, unlike all the others, this woman's visits were long and continued for a long time—eight months, every single day.

"There is no doubt that she is suffering from some sort of disorder..."

"Perhaps she has gone mad," said one of the women.

This vicious accusation became known to Miriam, and she whispered to herself in a critical tone:

"Anyone who visits his mother's grave is crazy? They can go to hell!"

It was the only time Miriam had heard talk about her visits to the cemetery, yet she felt that the stares directed at her were stronger than words.

She no longer felt comfortable during her visits, and she began to attend the grave in the early morning hours while people were still asleep. But even that was difficult for her, for just the idea of having to visit her mother's grave in secret stirred oppressive thoughts within her

"I need counseling, professional help," she decided, and came.

After a brief conversation, I realized that there was no avoiding hypnosis in order to help her establish a connection with her mother so that she could hear her and, together, they could devise some advice on what to do.

She sat comfortably, closed her eyes, sank into the chair, and her body relaxed. While in a state of hypnosis, she held the following conversation with her mother:

... (silence–the mother says nothing)

"Mom, where are you?"

... (silence – the mother still says nothing)

"Ask her if she can hear you," I interjected into the conversation.

"She hears me."

"If so, then ask her why she isn't responding to you," I said.

"She's not pleased... she's angry." (She begins to tear up.)

"Why?" I asked.

"She can't speak."

"What would she say if she could speak?"

"Heal me... set me free... I'm not breathing," she said, and her crying intensified.

"Heal her... set her free," I requested of her.

"I can't... I can't... I can't," she said, and began hitting her head and convulsing.

"Alright... alright... breathe quietly... quietly... a quiet exhale and a quiet inhale... quietly... You are now in the safe place you told me about... that quiet place on the seashore... now... the sound of the gentle waves reaches your ears... tranquility reigns in the place... the tops of tall palm trees dance quietly... gentle breezes caress your face... now... and your hair... and your body... your body is relaxed and at ease... now... You are lying on the warm sand, feeling its warmth on your body, breathing quietly... quietly..."

Her body became limply relaxed, she stopped crying, and she began to breathe more peacefully and freely. After she calmed down, I continued speaking to her:

"It's hard for you to break free from your mother... It's hard for you to part from her... but your conscious understands that her physical death does not mean a spiritual death, nor does it erase those warm memories you share with her... You can let her go and allow her to leave, and afterward, whenever you wish, you can recall those memories you choose simply by closing your eyes and taking three breaths... Your subconscious will guide you and lead you to them... You can do this now and at any time you wish... just close your eyes and take three breaths, and feel tranquility and inner calm... You will also be filled with vitality and abundant energy to surge forward and accomplish the things you excel at in your work and your professional, personal, and social life... I now remember that girl you told me about, the one whose parents locked her up at home because of her disability, that girl who suffered from impairment, and whose parents believed that by confining her, they were protecting her, it didn't matter from what... Perhaps they wanted to believe that, and perhaps they wanted to soothe their conscience; in any case, the confinement did not help the girl nor save her from death... Perhaps we should ask ourselves: what did that girl want? To be free and liberated or to be confined? But in the end, she died, died while she was still a child... Perhaps she wanted to break free, and she did so through death... Imagine what would have happened if her parents could imprison her soul, just imagine... Your mother, Miriam, lived freely and died freely... Now she needs your help, especially now she needs you as she never did before... She needs you to set her free, to be released..."

Quiet tears, a light sweat on her face, slow and silent breathing. A long silence. I left her, or more precisely, I let her confront—with the aid of her inner subconscious—the fear of remaining alive after parting from her mother.

After a few minutes, when I sensed from her energy and the movement of her body that the session had come to an end, I asked her to return.

"How are you?" I asked her after she opened her eyes.

She sighed a little and said:

"I'm fine, my mother asked to be released, and I complied with her request. I love her and will continue to love her. Her memory will accompany me all my life. But what shall I do now?"

"Her memory and your memories of the warm moments with her will accompany you and be with you whenever you wish. Release her and free yourself, start living."

At their next meeting at the institution, Miriam looked into the eyes of the child's mother, who was diagnosed with a developmental intellectual disability, and saw in them a tranquil gaze and a deep silence. She is no longer troubled by questions such as: What will happen to this child when he grows up? How will he live his life? Will he die? Will he live?

The father continues to move his fingers, passing along the beads of the prayer string, and playing the role of the supporter, one who places his trust in God, who holds everything in His hands.

The mother gathered around her a group of other mothers at the institution, and they established contact with charity organizations and institutions that care for children with special needs. Moreover, they spread a message stating that these children have a full right to live with dignity, to marry, to have children, and to mature, and that they are loved just as they are.

Loved just as they are!

Miriam did not attend the third meeting we had scheduled. To me, it was a great loss, for in her liberating herself from her fears of loneliness and her continual search for a caressing hand and an eye to ensure her serenity, I saw a personal project that helped me address my own problems.

I considered talking to her about her relationship with her husband and decided to explore the possibility of referring them to couples therapy.

The important thing is that the goal for which she came was achieved, I tried to convince myself.

But I still heard the neighbors' whispers and felt their stares.

Chapter 9

Sami

WHO PASSED HIS STRESS ON TO HIS THERAPIST

Sometimes, it is enough that, through your surrender and your inability to provide treatment to the one seeking it, you help him.

He sits hunched over in small, enclosed restrooms. The cleaning worker passed by them in recent days, and the odor emanating from them mingled with the voices of children running and roaming outside. In his ears, the voices of teachers—admonishing—reach him, saying: "Oh, woe to you, child, be careful!" and "You, girl, pick up the paper from the ground immediately!" A group of children is playing outside, "Run, Doves," and another group is playing "Bill."

"Bill" is a game that, for a long time, captured his heart at the beginning of adolescence. What is put to the test in it is the level of trust that the player bestows upon his lungs, for if they betray him and do not supply him with enough air to express himself in one breath—without taking in air between—during an attack on the opponent's arena. He returns to his arena with the marks of the enemy's hands on his body from the many blows inflicted upon him, or worse, he becomes counted among those called "the dead" or "the captives." They are at the mercy of the opponent and wait in confinement for a fighter who will risk himself, and is strong, fast, and possesses dependable lungs containing a large amount of oxygen—enough to let him soar beyond the battlefield and breathe the spirit of freedom into those "dead" by touching their bodies and bringing them back to life.

He sits hunched over in the restroom, placing his head between his hands, listening — despite himself — to the voices that undermine his self-confidence, and wondering how far his fears of people and his distancing from them have reached. At times he longs to see them from afar, so he climbs onto the toilet and peeks furtively through the small, high window. But soon it becomes clear to him that he isn't missing much, and that the smell of the restroom is preferable to the odor emanating from the way people behave and their disgraceful treatment of one another. Yet sometimes he swallows his saliva, and a sensation of bitterness and sorrow grips him as he sees smiles on the faces of some of the children enjoying the game.

Every time, he sits in exactly the same posture, and although he does not have a clock to tell him the time, his heart always indicates it. And indeed, the sound of "The Commando," the bell, always reaches him precisely at the moment he expects it. He even begins to count backwards in his heart: ten, nine, eight, seven, six, five, four, three, two, one, and... his voice comes to his ears — beautiful and resonant, confident and strong — to free him from the imprisonment into which he entered "voluntarily" before he enters the second imprisonment, the classroom, which, of course, was not voluntary.

The transition from one prison to another grants him a few minutes to breathe freedom. Although the journey from the restroom to the classroom usually takes about two minutes, he always extends it. The students hurry into the classrooms, and the teachers on duty urge them to enter in an orderly manner, while he ambles back and forth during those moments. No one notices his presence, and no one pays any attention to him. The Arabs were right in their saying: "Put your head among the heads and say: O beheader," because his meandering among the crowd and the voices gives him great confidence.

Fulfilling his emotional needs in the restroom allowed him to feel secure within that small room, with its repulsive odor—which to others was offensive, but to him was the most natural scent. He became so accustomed to it that his senses were willing to accept it, and his brain reprogrammed its place within it.

This small room cares for him more than venturing out into the world. Not long ago, a war broke out in the neighborhood, known to us as a "brawl," in which nearly all the adults participated, and in which live weapons and clubs were used. In that war, his friend Rani, who was not even eight years old, was killed by a stray bullet... a stray bullet, we said!

He began his studies at this school a year earlier, after returning with his parents from the United States, where he was born and attended one of the elementary schools. He encountered many difficulties in adjusting socially and academically at this school, even though he was proficient in English. His problem was social and emotional, and he was described as someone who tended to isolate himself and minimize his social contacts. His father, who was engaged in commerce and amassed great wealth, invested tremendous efforts to help him. He enrolled him in many extracurricular classes, such as drama, theater, and swimming, with the aim of strengthening his personality and self-confidence and improving his social relationships. However, the results did not live up to these hopes.

Following a deep economic crisis that erupted in the United States and around the world in 2008, the family was forced to salvage its investments, transfer the shares and the money in its bank accounts—worth millions—to the homeland, and return there with no other choice.

Not only did the sudden move to another country and a new school add to his difficulties, but also an insufficient command of his mother tongue, since English had taken the place of Arabic as the main language of communication at home.

Here, as well, the parents left no stone unturned. They spent large sums of money on private lessons. They initiated and organized social events in their new, sumptuous home in the city in order to enhance their son's social connections and attract friends to him. However, peers of his age exploited this inexhaustible treasure that fell into their path and increased their ridicule of him, both to his face and behind his back.

My friend, who is a professional psychologist, once asked me if I could treat a person suffering from chronic anxiety using hypnosis.

"Certainly," I answered her.

This was after I had already begun practicing hypnosis, driven by the belief that nothing can stand against its influence—and I still believe that.

"This guy is the son of one of my friends; he is studying at the university. I began treating him three months ago, and I am not sure if I can help him. He came to me after a period of irregular treatment by a psychologist. That treatment did not yield results, and his condition did not improve. It's possible that my relationship with his mother affected the treatment process. I thought that perhaps hypnosis might help him."

She said this hesitantly, and I sensed the apprehension behind her words. She was likely attempting to "get rid" of the young man, since by nature, no one likes to fail.

I did not expect him, as the appointed time of his arrival had not yet come.

It was our first meeting. I saw him through the clinic window, stepping out of his new Audi, and my curiosity was aroused. He wore dark sunglasses, even though at that moment the sun had already hidden behind the clouds. It was a spring day in February, about which it was said:

"Capricious February – even if it rains, the aroma of summer is present."

Usually, I stand by the window for a few moments between therapy sessions, breathing in fresh air and releasing a deep sigh and a long exhalation to discharge everything that had accumulated within me during the previous session. Sometimes I fail to set up a mirror between myself and the person sitting across from me to reflect his feelings — which are often laden with deep suffering — and I cannot avoid the feelings of empathy that are sometimes so strong they transcend mere understanding.

I observe, through the window, the events unfolding in the neighborhood and the behavior of drivers and people in general. In those few minutes, I sink into a kind of hypnotic trance and detach from the world in order to reclaim my energy. Observing people's behavior is a habit to which I have become addicted, and I love that addiction. I do not agree with the saying "He who watches people will die of sorrow." I watch people's behavior and try to understand the reasons for the differences in their ways and their varied responses to similar events. In reaction to the same event, one might smile, another gets angry, a third ignores it, and a fourth pulls out a knife. In short, I love to observe people and to collect new events to analyze them. One might say it is an obsessive curiosity.

This observation calms me, as it is a form of release and a kind of therapeutic introspection that I adopted long ago.

He got out of his car with movements that struck me as calm, restrained, and confident, and as I observed him, I ruled out the possibility that I was his destination. Usually, I manage to mentally paint the external appearance of my clients through a phone conversation or the information I had previously received about them. But Sami—that was his name—surprised me when he knocked on the clinic door and entered.

"Okay," I said to myself, "I am facing a challenge. I failed to sketch his persona; it will be interesting to see how the treatment unfolds."

Perhaps I inadvertently created a suggestion for myself, thinking that I was facing a situation that was unique and more complicated.

"Please, have a seat," I told him after he sat down without waiting for my invitation. He placed his car keys and his mobile phone on the table and lifted his sunglasses onto his head.

"Doctor, as I told you on the phone, I am stressed, very stressed," he said, while fixing his gaze on my eyes as if searching for something.

"Alright, I understand that you are eager to begin describing the reason that brought you here. But first, let me collect some personal details from you."

"My name is Sami, as I told you on the phone. I am a fourth-year medical student at the university in Jerusalem. My problem is that I am always stressed."

"Aha, I understand. You sometimes feel stressed. But tell me, please, how old are you?" I asked him to gauge his willingness to step away from his "stress" momentarily.

"I am 26. But what does my age have to do with the stress I'm under? I am seriously stressed. And not just sometimes—I am always stressed," he said, and it seemed his patience was about to run out.

"Alright, tell me since when you have been feeling this

stress," I asked him (stressed!) as I responded to him and went along with his tension.

"For a long time. I've been stressed for a long time. I miss exams and don't attend classes. I don't know... I am sooo stressed."

"Tell me, since when. When did you start feeling this stress?"

"Since I was in high school, before the final exams. And I'm still stressed to this day and don't know what to do. My entire life is one big stress—stress at school, stress at home..."

"And here as well. I hear your stress. I understand it and I feel it too."

He sighed, taking in a deep breath and exhaling the air as he looked at me with an intense gaze accompanied by a slight smile that struck me as odd—a smile whose meaning I only understood later.

When he hears the sound of his "commando"—the bell—he quietly returns to the classroom and takes his seat in the last row next to his friend Hakim, or "Abd al-Hakim" as his classmates mockingly call him.

Hakim (that was his real name) was not favored by luck, nor did he possess the intellectual abilities that would have allowed him to achieve academic success like his other classmates. However, he had a sturdy build, and his peers were afraid of him. Moreover, if anyone mocked him and called him "Abd al-Hakim," they would immediately run away in fear of his powerful kicks to their backs.

"What is your name?" asked the sheikh in a clipped tone

at the beginning of the year, after he had given his predecessor a "talking-to" for not knowing how to interpret the words of Surat al-Baqrah (the Chapter of the Cow in the Quran).

"Ha... ha... Hakim," he stammered in terror as he shifted his gaze between the sheikh's eyes and the long stick in his hand.

"Hakim?" asked the sheikh in bewilderment and mockery. "Hakim?!" he repeated, then declared resolutely, "Your name is Abd al-Hakim! Hakim (the wise) belongs solely to God, exalted be He."

He asked him to read aloud, and since he could not, he received four blows on his palms from a one-meter-long wooden ruler that served as an aid to the geometry teacher, accompanied by remarks delivered in a tone of skepticism and wonder, yet closer to ridicule:

"Hakim, he says... Hakim..."

In short, Sami found refuge with that Hakim, or Abd al-Hakim, while he was in class. Still, during the break, he preferred to sit in the restroom, for he did not want his classmates to see that he had any association with al-Hakim, who, apparently, was not as wise as his name would suggest, given that he had, as mentioned, a low intellectual capacity. Furthermore, he was unable to benefit from the possibility of receiving an appropriate psychological evaluation to place him in an educational setting that matched his abilities**.

When Sami was seven years old, he had a brother born under difficult circumstances that put their mother's life in great danger, and consequently, she had to remain in the hospital for several weeks. At that time, the family was visiting relatives in the "homeland," where she used to spend the entire summer vacation once every two years. While his mother was away from home, a brawl erupted in the neighborhood during which gunfire broke out. Rani, his friend, was killed as mentioned earlier, and his cousin was severely injured and nearly died from his injuries.

He told me that he wet the bed that very night, and also on the nights that followed.

When he recounted this tragic story of his childhood, a smile never left his face. His smile revealed dazzling white teeth and conveyed a concealed sorrow that grew stronger as he matured, exposing even more of his teeth.

During his middle school years, signs indicative of test anxiety began to emerge in him. Every time an exam appeared difficult, he would resort to crying as an escape and a means to avoid it. Nevertheless, he was an outstanding student, particularly in sciences, mathematics, and English, and consequently, the teachers treated him leniently during exam periods.

"Why is all this happening to me?" he wondered, "I can't imagine myself without stress."

"What do you mean by 'this'?" I asked.

"This...? It is the mountain that sits on my head," he replied.

I loved that metaphor he used so effortlessly.

"Nice," I said to myself, "let's see what the story is of that mountain that sits on your head."

From that point on, we continued our conversation after he entered a state of hypnosis.

His body was relaxed on the sofa; he stretched his legs forward, tilted his head back, and leaned on a comfortable spot atop a small cushion, ready and willing to sink into a hypnotic conversation based on the very metaphor he had chosen at the outset.

"Describe that mountain to me," I requested.

"A solitary, small mountain in the middle of a green plain that stretches far and wide."

"A solitary, small mountain... small in what sense?" I wondered.

"Small in age. It emerged, or rose, from the plain some time ago... perhaps ten years or a little more."

"A solitary, small mountain in the middle of a green plain... that rose about ten years ago... when you were a child... tell me, what else is there?"

"A train... I see a train approaching... a train moving along a railroad track... a long railroad track—I don't know where it comes from... but it seems that its route extends far beyond the mountain... the problem is that every time the train reaches the mountain, it stops... it doesn't continue."

"Aha, it doesn't continue," I attempted to encourage him to go on.

"The mountain does not allow it to continue."

"It seems that the mountain has its reasons for doing so," I said.

"The solitary mountain... standing alone... it captures anyone who passes by and does not let them continue."

Moments of silence...

The rhythm of his breathing grew faster. His head moved from side to side, and signs of tension became apparent on his body. His body language took the place of words, and he fell silent. A few moments passed during which I allowed him to deal with "the mountain, the train, and what lies between them" — and perhaps with other things as well.

"Where are you now?" I asked.

He did not answer.

"The solitary mountain on a green plain and a long railroad track running alongside it... There is a train there... tell me, where is that picture derived from?" I tried to bring him back to the point where he had left me. I did not want to allow him to drift alone in his imagination and thoughts for longer than the time allocated, as I bear professional responsibility. Besides, I was curious to know what was unfolding in his mind.

"I am on the train... alone... There are no people... the train stops and cannot continue... it wants to continue, but something holds it back... binds it... shackles it with a strong rope."

Tears began to well up in his eyes, and his voice was scarcely audible.

"And the mountain?"

"I don't know... I'm trying... I want to run away... to move on... but it doesn't let me... I can't." Here, he began speaking in the first person, as if he himself were the train.

"Have you ever spoken with it? I mean, with the mountain?"

"No."

"Do you want to release the rope or check with the mountain why it binds you... The train?"

"It says it wants people to come to it... to entertain it."

"Aha, it wants people to come to it to entertain it, and that is why it holds onto whoever passes by and does not let them go."

"So what? I can go back to visit him," he said to himself, as if he had found an excuse to persuade the mountain to release him and untie the rope.

"Okay, tell him that," I said.

The conversation between him and me, and between him and the train and the mountain, continued for a long time, during which he promised the mountain that he would visit it at every possible opportunity.

Finally, Sami... pardon... the train was released, and it continued on its way. Through the side mirror, Saami saw how the mountain began to recede as the train moved away... it receded... and how the mountain gradually became smaller and smaller.

I gave him several post-hypnotic suggestions, through which his ability to engage in dialogue and arrive at solutions each time he felt "bound" became apparent. I explained that he might be surprised by his ability to release the ties in the ropes of stress, and he might marvel at the speed with which he reaches "solutions" to the difficulties and daily problems he encounters and may encounter in the future. Afterwards, I provided him with clear instructions on how to exit the hypnotic state and return to reality.

I attached great importance to addressing the source of this "stress," as Saami called it, through hypnosis. The abreaction (emotional catharsis) that occurred during the hypnosis constituted a crucial step in this process. For me, and from experience, it was enough for Sami to feel even a slight drop in the level of stress he had carried for many years.

But in the next session, he surprised me when, immediately after replying to my greeting without waiting for any instruction from me, he said:

"There has been no improvement in my condition, Doctor. I'm still stressed. I don't see that this hypnosis is producing any results. It's all just one big tension. I still can't make it to class and I don't complete anything. I'm stressed. Don't you see that I'm stressed? I wake up at night all tense, and in the morning, I feel terribly tired and can't get going. The stress is so overwhelming that I feel as though my head is about to explode. Just one enormous stress..."

I did not expect that. I did not expect that after three hypnotherapy sessions—during which I employed techniques I had always relied on that had never let me down, in addition to my scientific and theoretical knowledge, and not least the fact that I trust the unconscious and my intuition—he would come and declare this prolonged, constant "stress."

And I love to expect...

I began to feel stressed myself.

There, my first failure as a hypnotherapist had arrived.

We sat down to talk about the mountain, the rope, and the plain, about childhood and school, about the fight and his friend's murder, about the restrooms, and the game of "Bill." Meanwhile, I examined the secondary gain he might be deriving from his stress.

Sami responded openly to my words. He shared with me his memories and fears—and he wept. I practiced self-hypnosis with him and asked him to do it twice a day until our next session.

That was all I could do at that stage, I told myself; a change had to occur so that I could begin to address the "mountain" and examine the reasons for its creation, along with other matters that would undoubtedly arise during therapy.

In any case, the initial treatment of Sami's stress through hypnosis extended beyond the number of sessions I had expected, in which I thought I could reduce his stress to a minimum—the goal we had agreed upon in our first session.

He arrived, even though the anticipated time for his arrival had not yet come.

It was his sixth time. I saw him through the clinic's window, stepping out of his new Audi—the very car he had used to come to our first session. Once again, he sparked my curiosity. He put on those same dark sunglasses, even though at that hour of a spring day in April the sun was hidden behind the clouds.

He emerged from his car with movements that struck me as calm, measured, and confident—exactly as he had on the first occasion—and he instilled in me a sense of tension. Déjà vu... When I first saw him, I hadn't expected to see him as he truly was, but now he had come, and I did not know what awaited me.

He placed his car keys and his mobile phone on the table, and he rested his sunglasses on his head just as he had during our first meeting.

"Doctor, there's been no improvement with me. I'm still stressed. Extremely stressed. The treatment isn't helping me. It turns out that this hypnosis isn't helping at all," he said, casting a look into my eyes as if searching for something.

What is he searching for? Why does he always come to me with such bad news? I did what I knew and what was supposed to bring about change, even a simple change, in the state of stress he was in, but every time he comes back, telling me that I've failed. In fact, I had failed even before he stepped into the clinic for the first time, when I couldn't imprint his image in my mind, before I'd observed him from the window. What kind of curse is this? I thought to myself, blaming myself for my intuition betraying me. I felt terribly awful, and my own stress grew.

Am I the cause, or is it him? Perhaps both? And maybe it is the hypnosis?

It occurred to me that perhaps the foundations of this "mountain" are deeply rooted in history, and that this "train" comes from the distant past; therefore, one must dig deeper and go far back to understand what is happening today.

I felt I was on the verge of surrender, and I decided to flow with the signs I received from the unconscious and its guidance. I did not seek a theoretical source or a psychological school of thought to justify and interpret for myself what I was about to do.

I decided to continue trusting the unconscious and to listen to its voice on the assumption that it was undoubtedly trying to help me—and that I wasn't permitting it to do so... of course... after all, I had given myself a suggestion, even before the first therapeutic session began, sincerely and unknowingly, that the situation would be complex and convoluted and that there was a chance I would fail.

I sat down facing him after he had entered a state of

hypnosis, closed my eyes, and listened intently to the inner voice in a final attempt to help him... and myself.

"Listen to me, Sami," I said to him in a calm tone, "When I took you on for treatment, I had no doubt that I was capable of addressing your prolonged complaints through hypnosis and alleviating the stress that, by your own admission, you have endured for years. Your classmates and friends haven't managed to ease your burden. You were in psychological therapy for about two years, with no improvement in your condition. You turned to cognitive-behavioral therapy with biofeedback and tried it for several months, but it yielded no results. The stress you experience is immense, and it seems it will continue to accompany you as long as you feel that those around you either do not notice it, ignore it, or truly fail to understand it. You need someone who sees you, who sees the suffering that sometimes manifests in this tension. It is a great stress... even exceedingly so... Every time those around you disregard your suffering, you feel profound disappointment, frustration, and perhaps even anger... There is something within you that causes this stress to blaze up even more in order to be seen—to stand out so that others notice it, admit they were wrong, and show understanding for the suffering you endure; to empathize with you, accept you, love you... Yet in truth, none of those you wish would understand you truly comprehend you. This matters greatly to you—it is vital for you to prove this suffering and the existence of this stress so that your loved ones see you... Well then, here is the testimony of a respected therapist attesting that your stress is great. And here is the testimony of another therapist you approached who did not help you. That testimony too confirmed that your stress is great. Now, there remains the testimony of a hypnotherapist... and I too say to you that your stress is great, Sami... so great that hypnosis by itself is incapable of overcoming it... but as you know from previous sessions, the only one who can alleviate your stress and suffering is you. That is your inner voice. It is your unconscious. It contains all the strengths and all the possibilities needed to deal with everything happening to you and to address it... Your unconscious tells you now, right now, at this very moment... that you are strong... you can do it... and just as you overcame your first therapist, so will you conquer this stress... just as you overcame your second therapist, so you can control the stress... just as you transferred your stress to your third therapist — me — and managed to unsettle him, so too are you capable of controlling this stress... From now on, you will no longer have to prove to anyone that you are stressed. From now on, you will understand that the "squeezings" in the restrooms are over. You are free, you are completely liberated... You will feel secure in the yard, at the university, in the street, at home, in your neighborhood, everywhere. This sense of security will accompany you in every step you take. That stress has fulfilled its role after loyally serving and protecting you in your youth when you needed it. From now on, the stress will be at a normal, healthy level — you won't need it with the same intensity anymore... From this moment on, you are free from it. You are liberated from it. You will be able to socialize with others, share with some of them your difficulties, your thoughts, your genuine feelings. From now on, express your feelings as they are. Today, you are genuine... Your emotions are sincere; express them as they are... The more honest you are with yourself, the greater inner peace and self-satisfaction you will feel. As you see yourself, so will others see you... If you treat yourself kindly, those around you will treat you with kindness. If you love yourself and send love to those around you, then they will love you, and you will feel inner tranquility and calm. From now on, it is solely in your hands. You are capable, you can do it!"

He sighed, taking a deep breath and exhaling. A tear rolled down from his right eye, accompanied by a gentle, pleasant smile.

It was the smile of victory.

I quietly brought him out of hypnosis after counting to ten and giving him the instructions to awaken. I reinforced him with a few affirmations about victory, strength, and the sense of satisfaction with his condition.

He opened his eyes, wiped the tears from his cheeks, sighed deeply, and fell silent.

Perhaps that "victory" required my testimony about his stress. Transferring his power within him was essential.

And most importantly, in the end, he overcame himself and freed himself.

Thus, the treatment was over. In fact, I only understood what had happened after I presented this situation at a workshop held as part of one of the conferences I attended on the subject of hypnosis.

If the therapist does not overcome his ego, there is no chance that the patient will free himself from his suffering!

Chapter 10

His name is Saeed (happy)

and he is anxiety-ridden

A case of stage fright

Tuesday, April 15, at five minutes to ten in the morning.

He hears the sound of a bell he does not want to hear, sighs, and with heavy steps makes his way to the lecture hall at the university. His eyes are red, his eyelids puffy, his lips dry, and he carries his large body with evident difficulty.

His heart is pounding rapidly, and he is unable to think in those moments to understand what is happening in his body, what is coming from his mouth, and what is occurring around him. He does not know whether his thoughts have gone silent because of cortisol and fear, or because of the alcohol in his bloodstream, or the combined effect of the two. Perhaps his "breakfast"—two sips of Red Label whiskey gulped on his way to the university—had taken effect more than he intended.

In fact, he does not know if, after those two sips, he went on to have a third, or even a fourth. He does not remember and cannot recall. There is no doubt that the alcohol affected his consciousness, yet the fear that gripped him was even stronger. The amygdala in his brain awakened to confront that threat, lacking any form, color, or sensation. It seems that his prefrontal cortex was no longer functioning as required and did not activate his reasoning; in those moments, his general mental faculties no longer had the strength to perform their roles.

He knows this well. He knows that when he is faced with any threat or gripped by fear, the amygdala begins to respond to that event and accelerates the release of hormones—such as cortisol—that aid in the survival fight. A similar process occurs in all living beings, except that nature has endowed humans with a prefrontal cortex that moderates fear and provides it with a rational dimension once it activates the kind of thinking that, according to brain researchers and anthropologists, is unique to humans alone.

But if that is so, why does a person behave like an animal when he senses any threat to his ego? Why does he rush to pull out a knife or a gun and kill?

What is the role of the prefrontal cortex about which scientists speak?

In any event, this is not our subject here. It is a philosophical and scientific topic with a myriad of differing opinions and interpretations. It concerns, for instance, a person who says one thing and acts oppositely. He always calls for tolerance, yet does not refrain from eliminating someone with a word, a glance, or through indifference—even with violence.

All that interests him now is to find a way out of the predicament his lecturer imposed on him, to uphold his commitment and present his assignment to his class in a few minutes.

Two weeks before that, precisely on April 1, his lecturer had asked him to prepare for submitting the final assignment and to present it to the students. Upon hearing this request, he was overwhelmed by a feeling of suffocation and could scarcely breathe. He felt as though his lungs were contracting and shrinking, not supplying him with enough oxygen, nor taking in enough air. Had it not been for his ribcage, which embraced him lovingly, his heart would have burst out and fled his body while he cried out in sheer exertion. His ears turned red. The many glasses of water he drank failed to quench his thirst or moisten his mouth and lips, and if that wasn't enough, beads of sweat trickled down from his forehead. He felt in his stomach a rumbling that aroused in him an acute desire to rush to the restroom.

It was the first time he had been gripped by such fear.

"God! As if the lecturer enjoyed tormenting me. To hell with him! He could have completely freed me from this. I am the ever-dependable and diligent student on whom he often relies."

On that day, he returned home and couldn't fall asleep. All he sought was to feel a little security and to hide from stares filled with shame. He did not want a certificate, nor an instruction, nor air contaminated with fear and anxiety. He was searching for a way to protect himself from this looming storm. He needed much more time to prepare for it, yet he knew that even if he had all the time in the world, he wouldn't feel ready. He felt an urgent need to tighten his clothes around his body and to tighten his tie so that it couldn't be removed, not even by himself. He could not understand his own soul or treat it with leniency in such circumstances. He would place it before him, scowl at it, sometimes raising his index finger and sometimes his hand in reproach, and soon became angry with it for its silence, beginning to punish it with a barrage of stones or a beating as if it were a whore that had cheated on him.

He had to protect himself from himself.

Despite his many successes in life in general and in his studies in particular, his relationship with himself had always been marked by a negative attitude. His self–estimation and appraisal of his abilities never matched the objective data or what people said about him. Every time he stood before the mirror, he saw nothing but an ugly, wretched, and worthless man. He suffered from a self–perception that was empty of substance, and he exerted every effort to hide it. He believed that he had generally succeeded, yet he felt threatened by the danger looming before him and was convinced that he was about to expose his shameful truth to his classmates.

That very night, memories carried him back to the day when his Arabic language teacher punished him while he was in ninth grade, and he left the school never to return.

It was an Arabic culture class, and the subject was etched into his memory: one of Al-Hajjaj bin Yusuf's speeches[6]

"Saeed, read!" the teacher suddenly commanded him.

Saeed looked at the teacher and shrank in his place, trying to disappear.

"Uh... uh... me, um... teacher?"

"Yes, you! What's wrong with you? Why are you sitting like that? Read!" the teacher said in a clipped tone.

Saeed fixed his eyes on the words written before him:

"I am a famous and experienced man; when I wrap the imamah (the headscarf) around my head, I become recognized..."

His heart pounded wildly, his blood pressure soared, and his cheeks and ears burned. He knew these lines well—he even had them memorized—but he could not bring them out of his mouth.

"I just need to begin; then everything will fall into place", he thought to himself.

He searched within himself for a way to fluently articulate the letter "Alef"—the very challenge that had been set at the start of the speech. The speech demanded eloquence, self-confidence, good rhetoric, a piercing eye, and a sharp tongue, while he had suffered from a stutter since childhood.

He mumbled the speech to himself without anyone else hearing him. The problem lay not in the pronunciation of the words but in his self-confidence. The more he tried to conceal the stutter within him, the more it betrayed him, finding an outlet and inviting mockery and ridicule. Instantly, he envisioned voices of laughter echoing around him—laughter that reverberated repeatedly during card games at his schoolmates' houses.

He examined himself in silence, turned the page in the book before him, and then replaced it in an attempt to gain a few moments to steady his tongue and the movements of his mouth, to confront himself and begin reading. He drew a deep breath, exhaled quickly without turning his head to either side, and saw dozens of eyes quietly following him, waiting for the moment when they would burst into laughter. He saw them lurking around him, eager to pounce in order to have a bit of fun and to rouse themselves from the obvious stupor that had seized them at that noon hour, further compounded by the dryness of the lesson. The lack of culture in that culture class was about to join the gloomy mood of the teacher, whose low and nasal voice sounded as if God had composed only a single note on the musical scale.

Saeed refused to be the savior, refused to be the clown, and that added pressure upon pressure.

He challenged himself.

He began to practice silently, searching for a way to produce the very first sound and to start with "I...". But the word refused to emerge.

Several moments passed in a deadly silence as everyone awaited the emergence of words from his mouth, his eyes fixed on the book and his lips searching for a safe place to begin speaking. He felt the teacher's gaze pinned on him and the stares of his classmates fixed on him from every direction.

A few more moments passed, his mental pressure mounting and his face flushing. He began to feel heat emanating from his ears and quietly battled within himself to find a solution... to try... just the beginning, after which the words would flow spontaneously.

At the moment he began:

"...a famous and experienced man..."

The teacher interrupted his words:

"From the beginning, Saeed."

Saeed did not respond.

"I told you from the beginning. What's wrong with you? 'I am a famous man... I... I!!! Why did you jump ahead?"

Saeed did not respond.

The teacher looked at him, and a smile mixed with a hint of ridicule and scorn appeared on his face. He was a unique teacher—a skilled hunter who seized every opportunity to "catch" a student and subject him to mockery and ridicule before the entire class. All the students burst into laughter, both out of fear and a desire to please him, while he puffed up like a peacock that had satisfied its desires. Woe to the student who fell into that trap, and now someone had indeed fallen.

But Saeed was not willing to be prey.

"I... I... don't w–w–want to read, teacher!" he said loudly, his eyes wide and his face scrunched up as he swallowed his saliva. He knew what the consequences of his refusal would be. He understood that the battle with the teacher had begun, and that he was to blame for standing up to him, for not remaining silent, for finally declaring that he would not be a victim.

"What did you say?!"

"I don't want to read!!!" he said in a loud, clear voice without any stutter. Suddenly, he felt the words flowing from his mouth without any restraint.

"Yes, I don't want to read!" he repeated emphatically, and a few faint smiles appeared on his classmates' faces.

The teacher caught on to what was happening and realized that he was facing a confrontation—someone was challenging his authority— and he smiled.

"No, you do want!" the teacher retorted forcefully.

A few moments of silence passed, and Saeed felt a heat

breaking out all the more powerfully on his face and ears, as cortisol seized every cell in his body and adrenaline reigned on the battlefield. He was confronting him! His heart raced, and blood flowed powerfully through every fiber of his being. His anger had never flared up like it did at that moment.

"He doesn't know me... I'll show him!" he murmured to himself in a menacing tone.

"Alright, get out. Get out... d–d–don't w–w–want to r–r–read, is that what you're saying? Go out and wait for me by the principal's office," the teacher said mockingly.

Thus ended his first chapter. Those were Saeed's last moments at that school.

He left and never returned.

The teacher's angry, mocking stares followed him, and the smiling, sneering whispers of his classmates swirled around him.

And there were also a pair of sad, understanding, and loving eyes—eyes that radiated embarrassment and shame every time he perceived them in the recesses of his mind. They were the eyes of his beloved, which, whenever they met his gaze, would shy away with love and longing.

So unbearable was the shame in front of his beloved, and so cruel the exposure of his true self to her.

This scene flashed before his eyes repeatedly that night in early April.

"No, I will not go back there ever again," he told himself,

and vowed to make peace with himself and to defend his identity.

That night was undoubtedly very fruitful, and during it, he found a solution.

"Great, I know the way — even though I abandoned it long ago. That's what I'll do!"

And he fell asleep with a spark of hope in his heart.

Two weeks passed in the blink of an eye. He spent most of the time planning and contemplating, and he kept repeating words to himself that plunged him into a state of deep hypnosis:

"No, it's not possible without alcohol... It's not possible... It's not possible... It's not possible..."

Tuesday, April 15, one minute before ten in the morning.

The bell rang for the second time, announcing the start of the lecture. The ringing did not cease until the lecturer stood in the hall and waited for the last of the students to arrive.

"Damn the bell, and damn the lecturer who is never late," he muttered to himself while cursing himself and everyone.

"There's no chance I'll succeed. I'll surely stutter, and they'll laugh and mock me. I'm worthless, I'm a f–f–failure..."

Those were some of the words he repeatedly told himself. Their bitterness and severity grew and plunged him once again into a state of negative hypnosis — a state in which he expended great energy.

So bizarre was this negative self–hypnosis trance that he often lashed out at himself and gave in.

With great difficulty, he dragged himself and stood before a sea that seemed tumultuous to him, with waves rising and falling. Many similar, expressionless faces followed him — faces with large eyes that observed him for a moment, only to vanish and reappear elsewhere, to his right and left, in front of him and behind him, both far away and very near. They were in his thoughts, inside his head. They were eyes that sought to tear his clothes and penetrate his defense mechanisms, so that he might return to being that helpless and naked child as he emerged from his mother's womb.

He began to sway like a tall tree with a fragile trunk tossed by the wind. His voice would rise, then fall silent, sigh, and return softly and faintly. Every sound that emerged from him was like the wail of the sea, poised to swallow him.

This state persisted for a few moments that seemed like an eternity.

Suddenly, a voice he knew well approached him, and a large hand patted his shoulder.

"Alright, Saeed. Enough. You can return to your seat or go home to rest."

It was the voice of the lecturer, speaking in a calm and empathetic tone.

He was in the early part of his fourth decade. The eldest of three siblings, from a middle–class family. His father worked in one of the factories, and his mother was a seamstress, working from home sewing women's clothes. Saeed was married and had two daughters, the eldest of whom was not yet ten. From the information we received, it became clear that he had been a shy and introverted student. His social connections were limited, and he interacted only with his two brothers and with one of the neighbor's children who was three years his junior. As a result, he was referred for a psychological evaluation, which indicated an average intellectual capacity within the norm, with an IQ of 93. His level of functioning was relatively low compared to his intellectual potential, which was unfulfilled due to emotional issues and low self–esteem. In middle school, the teachers began to complain about behavioral problems, although his academic achievements were good. In high school, he attended for only three months before leaving, due to that same confrontation with the literature teacher.

After he stopped his studies, he would wander in the evenings through the lower neighborhood of the village, hoping to catch a glimpse of his beloved sitting on the balcony or standing behind the small window of her room. Every time he saw a moving figure in a house, his heart skipped, and he felt as though her warm presence enveloped him and her enchanting smile embraced him. He had not seen her since the day the literature teacher expelled him from class, and although he did not doubt that he loved her, he never revealed his love to her for fear of embarrassment.

He would pass by her house and walk as if heading toward some destination in the neighborhood, and every time he happened upon someone by chance, he felt deep inside that he must explain his presence there. Even though no one ever blocked his way or asked him anything, he would still see eyes hovering around him, tracking his every move. To himself, he thought that his behavior was repulsive and that it was shameful on his part to furtively peep at girls.

"But I don't spy on them. All I want and dream of is to see her, even if just for a moment," he told himself in an effort to defend his honor.

He loved walking in places where her footsteps once fell, on the earth that had brushed against the soles of her little shoes, to catch a scent that reminded him of her, and perhaps to hear her voice calling for her mother. It occurred to him that if luck were on his side, he might suddenly encounter her as she made her way back home from somewhere.

The moment he envisioned such a chance encounter, he became instantly anxious. Even if they were to cross paths, he wouldn't have the courage even to greet her or to look into her eyes. Yet it was enough for him if she saw him and felt the lingering breeze in her wake as it drifted by and embraced him.

He was afraid to share his love with her.

His love for her— for Layla—was his deepest secret.

A few months after he left the school, he heard from a friend a piece of news that shocked him.

"Did you hear that Layla got engaged and is about to get married?"

"Whaaa?!"

"They told me that her wedding will take place next Saturday. She's marrying a man from Haifa who is much older than she is." Upon hearing the words, his world went dark. He began running toward the lower part of the neighborhood, perhaps hoping to catch a glimpse of her from afar and cast one last look. He wanted to shout with all his might that he loved her, but fear and stuttering held him back, and his heart fell silent, unheard by anyone. He watched her house from a distance and saw figures and shadows here and there — a person on the balcony and darkness behind the window. In the end, he grew weary and burst into tears.

Judgment Day arrived, and he distanced himself from the village, sitting on the dividing fence by the road leading to Haifa, waiting to bid farewell to her.

A few cars passed by, whistling in a chorus of sounds. Gradually, they receded, their voices fading little by little as the fire in his heart blazed ever more intensely.

He saw no one, yet in his mind's eye he saw her, dressed in white and crying.

He burst into prolonged, unhesitating tears without a stutter.

From that day onward, Layla vanished.

They described him as a sensible fellow, albeit lazy. Shortly after leaving high school, he turned to religion and began spending long hours at the mosque. While still young, his parents pressed him to get married. "A strong woman takes care to uphold her husband," they said. And so it was.

Two years after his marriage, his first daughter was born. His wife, several years his senior and like a second mother to him, encouraged him to complete high school at an Arab school. He finished his studies, and the average of his final grades enabled him to pursue Organizational Consulting and Business Administration at the university.

"I want to be a 'businessman'," he used to say.

He loved the university at which he studied after battling life's hardships and maturing both intellectually and behaviorally. He gained social experience and managed to break through the barrier of fear he felt toward the villagers he knew.

The stuttering that had accompanied him in school had vanished, until that very moment revived what he had struggled to forget. "This lecture is cursed," he said.

He realized that he had a hidden problem now reemerging in a different form—and that he needed help.

He tried to seek help via one of the internet search engines, and after reading what he found, he concluded that he suffered from what is called "stage fright," the stuttering being merely one of its symptoms. He attempted various methods to cope, including personal coaching through exercises advised by the different participants on the websites he visited.

He tried to convince himself that this fear was nothing more than a thought born of the devil's tricks, and that he should neither heed it nor act upon it. He was to combat it by repeatedly reading Hadith[7] and passages from the Qur'an. However, all those attempts failed, and his condition not only did not improve, it worsened.

He attempted relaxation exercises, but immediately after closing his eyes, he saw before him faces that were jesting, mocking, and laughing—and he ran for his life.

His despair grew, and he felt utterly helpless. One thought tormented him: What will they say about me? Surely they will say, "This man is lost, a failure—nothing good will ever come of him."

There was one single question regarding the great

problem he now faced: How will he overcome this fear? Will he run away? Will he cower?

"No. My name is Saeed, and I am Saeed,[8] I am strong... What a disgrace! I am ashamed of myself. I am capable, I am strong, I am Saeed — but I am not happy, I am a coward, I am... and yet they still call me Saeed (happy). I am nothing."

And so he continued talking to himself.

It was a dialogue between attack and retreat. The retreat, the flight, and the surrender overwhelmed him.

"It will be alright; with two sedative pills, everything will be fine," he tried to convince himself.

Tuesday, April 22, at 9:15 in the morning.

It was the second and final deadline set by the lecturer for him to present his assignment to the students. He went to the pharmacy where one of his friends worked, consulted with him about a suitable medication, and the pharmacist sold him some pills and advised him:

"Take one pill half an hour before the lecture."

He followed the advice and swallowed one pill; then he waited a few moments, feeling no change in his mental state. A minute passed, then two, then three... as if hours had gone by. No change came, and his anxiety only increased. With just a few minutes left before his confrontation began—and he was still not ready—he swallowed another pill. After a few moments, his anxiety grew even more, for he still felt no difference. Finally, he swallowed a third pill and entered the hall.

There remained a quarter of an hour until the lecture began.

Suddenly, he felt a wave of relaxation, intense physical weakness, and an overwhelming need to sleep. Unable to stand, he sat down on a chair in the hall. Although he didn't hear the bell ring, he noticed students entering the hall one after another or in small groups, whispering, laughing, and discussing various matters. Each took his seat, preparing to listen to three short lectures by their peers. The lecturer entered and called on Saeed to be the first. Saeed began his lecture, yet remembered nothing of it. He turned to his presentation and read it word for word in a voice he barely heard. Suddenly, his voice vanished; he felt the words were not coming from his throat. He looked around in bewilderment, but saw no one, heard not the sound of crashing waves, nor did he see any faces peering from the hall's heights. In truth, he saw neither a hall nor an audience, but only heard murmurs here and there and soft bursts of laughter as if emanating from a dry, deep, dark well. The intensity of those voices overwhelmed him and brought him back to that famous speech of Al-Hajjaj bin Yusuf.

The lecturer requested to meet with him after the lecture and recommended that he seek psychological counseling.

He completed his master's degree while grappling with unspeakable psychological torment. Every time he was asked to give a lecture, he tried to evade it — sometimes succeeding, and sometimes having to resort to sedative drugs, to which he seemed to have grown addicted. He used them during his university studies, later in his work as an administrative manager at one of the small local organizations, each time he was required to present an annual report before the general council.

The psychological treatment recommended by the lecturer lasted for two years, but it did not help him, partly because he couldn't continue it due to the heavy expenses. Now he was on the verge of accepting the job he had long dreamed of—CEO of a large marketing company in the region. However, aware of the personal responsibility resting on his shoulders and the effects of the sedative drugs, he decided to try another form of psychological treatment, one through hypnosis.

"I want to break free from my fears and also from the sedative drugs," he said when he called me and asked to set up an appointment.

He came to me when he was thirty-three, dreaming of advancing and providing for himself and his family.

A tall man with a robust physique that appeared older than his years, half-bald, and meticulous about grooming his long mustache, which completely covered his upper lip. His appearance testified to careful, even extravagant, grooming. He wore a white shirt and neatly pressed black trousers.

He entered the therapy room with a smile that revealed yellowish teeth arranged in impeccable order.

After I signaled him to sit, he settled into the special chair and preempted me with a question about the "gong" in the room.

"What is that? It seems you take things very seriously," he said with a smile.

"Hi," I replied, and waited for him to continue.

And indeed, what I had anticipated occurred, and I moved toward him.

"Look, I lack nothing. Praise be to God — I have a master's degree, a loving and wonderful family, and a respectable livelihood."

"I see... You mean that you have nothing missing..."

"But... I don't know what else to tell you besides what I mentioned on the phone. I have stage fright. Brother, I don't know what happens to me when I stand before people. I must address this problem. I've read about hypnosis, and I believe only you can help me," he said hesitantly.

"I am sitting in a quiet, dark room, watching the romantic film 'Message in a Bottle' starring Kevin Costner, Robin Wright, and Paul Newman. My wife went to visit her parents, and I was left alone. I prepared a kettle of coffee for myself. It's cold outside. The room is on the second floor and contains a small writing desk and an air conditioner that, for most of the year, runs only a few days because the weather in this area is generally mild. There are no curtains on the windows, for I like to look outside without anything obstructing my view. From the southern window, I see in the distance Jabal al-Jermak (Mount Meron) and the green trees that cover it. From the northern window, I see the olive trees that crown the nearby hill. There, among the olive trees, stands a large, ancient carob tree — perhaps hundreds of years old. Sometimes I like to go there, especially when I feel bored or when I wish to relax. I sit under the tree, smoke a cigarette, gaze at its branches, and listen to the rustling of the leaves. On the tree, a nest of wild pigeons renews itself regularly, and I have seen with my own eyes many fledglings take flight from it."

It was Saeed's safe haven, where he felt at ease. More precisely, it was as if two safe places had merged into one: from the secure room in which he stayed, he would venture out to another refuge where the wild pigeons ceaselessly rebuild their nests and create new lives in safety and vibrancy.

He left the room for the tree and sat beneath it, then returned to watch "Message in a Bottle." I asked him to write a letter and place it in a bottle, and he chose to write about everything that stirred fears and worries within him. When I inquired what he intended to do with the letter and bottle, he replied that he would bury them in a far-off place where not a single human foot has trodden.

And that is what actually happened during the hypnotic induction (the initial phase of the hypnosis process), using the gong.

Once... twice... thriiiice

Gong... goooong... gooooooong...

"Now it is time for confrontation," I said, "You are entering the lecture hall at the university—the very hall where you delivered your first lecture... and your second... In this hall, you will release all your past experiences. You have carried them long enough, and now it is time to let them go... In this hall, where you faced your fears, you will relinquish all the experiences you have borne over the years, for you no longer need them. From this place, you will embrace new experiences that will become beautiful memories you will long to relive again and again... In this hall now sits an audience, waiting to hear your lecture, to hear from you all that you did not say back then."

I noticed that his body began to "speak" and express a sense of unease.

He is coping, I told myself.

"Good, Saeed... excellent... You are capable... well done!"

"I feel that my heart is beating strongly... as if it wishes to leave its place."

"Excellent... that is a positive feeling... your heart is racing... which means it is confronting... it is dancing... it is alive... it is strong."

He began breathing rapidly, moving his head silently from side to side, expressing a sense of discomfort.

"Now you are speaking before the audience, Saeed... you stand before them and speak... You pace back and forth on the stage... You see their eyes following you and looking at you with admiration... your speech is fluent, clear—a good, pleasant feeling... You are great... You are successful... This is a beautiful experience."

He calmed down slightly, yet his body continued to display a significant sense of discomfort. I decided to shift to the safe place:

"You are now sitting under the carob tree... the weather is pleasant... gentle breezes caress your face... your body... the scent of the tree permeates your nostrils... the wild pigeons' chicks chirp, perhaps wanting to share in your joy... You run your hand along the trunk of the tree and feel its firmness and the strength of centuries... You approach the portable gas stove and turn it on... the sound of crackling fire reaches your ears, and the flame dances with the gusts of wind... You set the kettle down... ahh... the aroma of the coffee rises to your nostrils... You sit in absolute comfort and drink your coffee. You are alone... You are free, breathing freely and at ease... You chose this place... You are in control of yourself, you are strong."

When I noticed that his body had relaxed, I continued to the second phase of the treatment, which would provide him with the tools to overcome the fear he was facing.

"You hold a remote control in your hand and watch your favorite movie. On this remote, there are two buttons – green and red – and by pressing them, you can manage your emotions, thoughts, and behavior, and control them. When you press the green button, you see beautiful images. You are sitting alone in your quiet room, just as you like, watching the romantic film 'Message in a Bottle'. Calm prevails in the place. Outside, it is cold, and pleasant breezes penetrate through the open windows. Perhaps you cast a glance from the movie outward and see Jabal al-Jermak in the distance and the green trees that cover it, or perhaps you decide to look northward and see the olive trees covering the nearby hill. There, among the olive trees, stands a large, ancient carob tree that seems to be hundreds of years old. Perhaps you decide to go there, sit beneath the tree, smoke a cigarette, observe its branches, and listen to the rustling of its leaves. You can see the nest of the wild pigeons. A pigeon hovers above – perhaps it wants to lay its eggs or feed its chicks, or maybe it is simply checking the state of the nest. You see your room and the carob tree, smell the aroma of coffee, and hear the rustling of the tree leaves and the cooing of the pigeons. You feel pleasure, confidence, and tranquility. When you press the red button, you see images accompanied by tension and anxiety, images you do not want to see. That is exactly the case. When you press the green button, you move to a safe place."

After repeating the experience of pressing the two buttons, the green and the red, while Saeed was still in a state of hypnosis, I returned with him to the first stage:

"Good, Saeed, now you can continue to strengthen your inner feeling and your self-confidence. You now feel complete tranquility... after you wrote the letter, put it in a bottle, and sent it to the place where it is meant to be. You now feel complete tranquility... With this wonderful feeling, you can imagine the remote for yourself, see the green button illuminating it... smiling at you... You remain with this feeling for a few moments, experiencing it in every detail... You see before you an audience of people looking at you and eagerly waiting for your words... You speak... speak about some subject... feeling that the words are flowing from your mouth in an absolutely unrestrained manner... with ease... Beautiful ideas and wonderful turns of phrase arise in your mind... You say them and see satisfaction and even astonishment in their eyes... they enjoy it... and you enjoy it too... A sense of calm spreads throughout your body, and you feel an energy flowing through every cell of you... through every limb... Now you look at the red button, press it, and feel tension and anxiety. You see before you a crowd and struggle to organize your thoughts and choose your words... You stutter a little... stutter even more... amid the onlookers, sounds of laughter are heard... Now you press the green button, and all of this stops... A sense of tranquility spreads through your body and takes over your thoughts... You are happy... You enjoy it... and in this way, you can control your thoughts, your words, and your self-confidence. You can control them with serenity, confidence, and ease when you press the green button on the remote... The green button is always before you and within your reach... it will be there whenever you wish... whenever you need it... just press it and everything will be all right."

After Saeed practiced transitioning from a state of tension to the opposite state of tranquility, confidence, and ease, and after he practiced controlling his emotions, I asked him to practice them at home as well, using the self-hypnosis he had worked on during the sessions.

"Every time you feel tense, you will see the green light smiling at you. All you have to do is press the green button... You will feel a calm and tranquility whose origin you cannot fathom... You too will smile and tell yourself how strong you are... how self-confident you are... how capable you are..."

Besides that, he was asked to face real-life pressure situations, to create a circumstance that would compel him to speak before a group of people, regardless of their number — the main point being to confront a situation that had eluded him until now. Naturally, he would be the one to determine the level of difficulty of the situation. He could start at a low level and speak before a group familiar to him, or at a higher level and speak before a large group of strangers.

It was a method of behavioral and supportive treatment using basic hypnosis, but by its very nature, it was not the only one.

He accepted the invitation to participate in the monthly meeting of the teaching staff at the high school he had left eighteen years earlier, and he parked his car in the schoolyard precisely at the moment when the bell signaling the end of the school day rang.

The place evoked mixed emotions in him.

Thoughts and bad memories brought him back to his school days. It was that very building from which he left for good on the day when the letter Aleph, with which Al-Hajjaj bin Yusuf insisted on opening his speech, got stuck in his throat. Additional memories also brought him back to his university days. It was the very same bell sound on the day when he staggered from his intoxication and was unable to stand steadily before his classmates.

He summoned the remote to him and saw the red button illuminated. The tension residing in him increased, and a strong desire to return to his home, to that safe place, arose within him. However, at that moment, he noticed the green light, and without realizing it, his finger moved toward it, and he pressed it, and smiled.

He took a few moments to fill his chest and stomach with air and exhaled it in a calm breath. He repeated this breathing three times, closed his eyes, and took out the virtual remote to ensure that the green button was still illuminated. He smiled once more, opened his eyes, and got out of his car.

He entered the principal's office, sat there alone to drink a cup of coffee and prepare for the meeting that was about to take place in the school hall. His heart pounded a little faster, and he broke into a light sweat under his arms. Nevertheless, he continued to focus on his breathing, drank some water, and held the virtual remote in his hand, with the green button continuing to glow, to calm him and assure him that everything would be all right.

After a while, the school principal entered his office and invited him to accompany him to a meeting during which he was to give a lecture on preparing an annual work plan. The trembling of his heart increased, but he reassured himself that everything would be fine, since the remote continued to govern his positive emotions. He entered the hall and stood before what seemed to him like a stormy sea, but soon it calmed down. Many faces looked at him and smiled—some appearing tired after a long day's work, others relaxed, but all awaited him eagerly.

He smiled to himself as he checked the remote and saw that it remained steadfast. He took one step to the right and another to the left and began to speak. His voice sounded clear, steady, and strong. Here and there, slight stutters accompanied him, adding strength to his words.

He continued speaking in this manner without knowing where his thoughts came from or from what source he was drawing his words. Silence reigned in the hall, and eyes that longed to hear him more intently were fixed upon him. He had no idea how much time had passed until he heard the principal's voice say:

"Mr. Saeed, you have exceeded the time allotted to you. Please try to finish your lecture."

He smiled and asked those present if they had any questions.

What we did during the treatment was sufficient.

For the next meeting, he came with a request to go back

in time using hypnosis, to that day when he could not recite the speech of Al-Hajjaj bin Yusuf.

He felt a strong need to correct the experience he had then and to prove to himself, to his mentor, and also to his beloved that he was capable and that he was strong.

And indeed, it was so.

Years passed since the brief treatment, during which Saeed never ceased sending me greetings from every person he met at a lecture, a conference, or a work meeting. He would ask them if they knew me and reveal to them the secret of his success at work today.

"It's the gong," he would say.

Chapter 11

Adel

Emetophobia–an uncontrollable fear of vomiting

During their very first meeting in the university lecture hall, he fell in love with her. A beautiful girl, short in stature and modest, whose glasses accentuated her face and whose short haircut added to her beauty.

He fell in love with her, but he did not know how to approach her.

He dreamed of her and imagined the touch of her gentle hand and her pleasant smile as she looked at him or embraced him. His love for her, his silence in her presence, and his reluctance to approach her made her heart flutter, and it occurred to her that he was nothing like those men who chase after every girl merely for entertainment and amusement, or to satisfy their narcissistic and masculine ego. He was different. Yet, she too did not have enough courage to approach him. She sent him soft, loving glances from afar and waited.

For his part, he waited for an opportunity, a savior, or an intermediary.

And she waited for courage.

The first year was coming to an end, along with the lectures, the discussions, the breaks, the morning and after-school meetings, the gatherings in the cafeteria where they conversed as two friends at their school bench, with eyes filled with a love that awaited only a verbal declaration. He did not understand, nor did she, why words necessarily had to be part of the expression of love. Wasn't a look, a heartbeat, or a moment of a "chance" meeting—though, in the name of fairness, transparency, and justice, it must be said that it was skillfully planned by both of them—enough?

Months passed, and he never had the chance to caress her hand, her face, and her short black hair.

Until an opportunity arrived, divinely orchestrated with the intention of helping them, and this time, it was a true coincidence.

They met in one of the cafés in the old city, far from the university, and they were alone, as the rest of their classmates were unable to make it there. He sat facing her and gazed into her eyes. In his heart, he said to her many things that he could have summed up in one sentence: "I have loved you since I first saw you." She gave him a questioning and expectant look: "Come on, man." He understood her glance, but the words were lost from his mouth. Suddenly, he felt nausea. He found no words to say to her, yet a volcano within him sought an outlet. He placed his right hand on his neck, unbuttoned the top button of his shirt, and, in an attempt to choke himself, pressed it. His eyes reddened and bulged from their sockets. He gave her a pleading, imploring look for help, turned his head to the right and left, swallowed his saliva, and shuddered with fear and shame.

He got up and ran to the restroom without apologizing to her, for opening his mouth at that moment would have been dangerous. Had he opened it, no words would have emerged because...

He ran toward the restroom. And she accompanied him with a look of empathy, pity, and helplessness...

She did not know how to shield him from the feelings of shame that she sensed emanating from him...

After he expelled his yellow bile, he returned to the table, ashamed and disheartened.

She was not there.

She had left.

After that meeting, fate no longer arranged for them to meet again, except in the lecture hall where he was either late or she was the first to leave.

A distant greeting and avoiding glances were enough for both sides.

He studied dentistry. During exam time, he would take a Dramamine pill against nausea an hour before the exam. After he finished his studies, he took this pill before heading to a job interview, a meeting, a social event, or any encounter with new people.

All the various and numerous medical tests he underwent every year since he was a high school student did not point to any medical reason for his condition.

But everything went smoothly. He would take a Dramamine pill in the morning, and his workday would pass without him vomiting. For extra precaution, he kept a plastic bag in his car in case he forgot to take the pill or the tension became too great, and he would need an extra pill that would not be within his reach.

His name is Adel and he is twenty-eight years old. Short in stature and of a stout build. He usually wears jeans and a white summer shirt. His hair is black, thick, and long. His eyes are large and slightly red, and their color is a light brown, like the color of honey.

He smiles a lot and rarely communicates through his gaze.

He is the eldest son, and he has two brothers. His father works in education. His mother was killed along with her friend in a traffic accident while they were on their way to a study day**. A truck swerved off its course, collided with the small Fiat in which they were traveling, and crushed it on top of its occupants. The rescue and fire brigade personnel struggled to extract the two bodies from the car. All their belongings – the bag they had with them, the notebooks, and the papers – got mixed up. He was then a ninth-grade student.

"What are the experiences you have been through, and are still going through, that your stomach cannot bear and 'process', and that it expels?" I whispered as I jotted down a few notes.

"Anyway, what must happen so that you won't vomit?" I asked him directly and unexpectedly.

"Maybe my stomach needs to grow a little. I feel it's small. And maybe there should be something to stop my food from rising upward."

"Your stomach is small?" I asked, bewildered.

"That is to say... it might be like the stomach of a twelve- or thirteen-year-old."

"In other words, like that of a ninth grader."

He did not respond.

"You said that maybe there should be something to stop your food from rising upward."

"Yes, something to block the esophagus."

"Like what, for instance? Describe that 'something' to me."

"... maybe a door... or a valve that opens when I eat and closes when I'm full."

"Describe it to me — what does it look like, what is it made of, where is it located, and how does it work?"

Adel described to me a small electric door located at the lower part of the esophagus, right next to the stomach's gateway, but he didn't know when and how it would be controlled and activated. He needed to devise a mechanism to manage this passage and open his door to allow the food to go in two directions – the first, using the force of gravity and the contraction and expansion that naturally pushes food downward, and the second, using mental tension and pressure to drive the food in the opposite direction, from the stomach upward.

Adel was a clever guy with a vivid imagination. I asked him to draw the stomach, the esophagus, and the door as he envisioned it, and then to simulate its opening and closing mechanism for himself.

The image of the digestive system he pulled from Google during our conversation helped him pinpoint more precisely the spot designated for this virtual gate.

And then the imaginative process paused, but only temporarily.

"How can we control and operate this gate?" I asked.

"Very simply, like the gate we have at home," he said, and showed me a black remote control hanging with his car keys, with a single button on it. When he pressed it, the home gate opened, and when he pressed it again, the gate closed.

You can imagine yourself walking in a forest. The weather is mild and warm. The path is narrow and just wide enough, perhaps, for two people walking close together. On both sides, tall trees rise, their colorful leaves falling gently to the ground. The scent of the earth after the first rain that fell last night drifts from every direction. The treetops sway quietly, and the mist upon them blends with the birds' songs to create a beautiful symphony that delights your ears. You walk alone. You can hear the sound of a waterfall nearby. Light droplets of water reach you quietly and caress your face. You stroll along the narrow stream, following the current and enjoying its pleasant babble... You feel an odd calm and a sense of security. You feel your body relaxing... at ease... You experience complete tranquility... You feel immense safety and inner well-being, and just as you are content, so is your stomach content... it expands... relaxes and grows. The more secure and calm you feel, the more your stomach expands and feels serene... it can contain what's inside it and all that enters peacefully... in its expansion, it guides the food within and pushes it into your intestines just as water flows smoothly along this small stream toward its next stations... just as the water flows forward, so does the food—only forward... this is the natural course of water in a stream... and the natural course of food in the intestines... and this state you surely recall that remote control that can operate cars, televisions, and gates... you imagine holding a remote in your hand, be it right or left... and in its center is one large button... by pressing it you can close the gate whenever you want... with another press you can open the gate whenever you feel the need to... but in reality you don't need to, because the biological process—thanks to gravity and the contraction and expansion of the esophagus—opens the gate spontaneously on its own. When you press the big button, you quietly close the gate to help the food continue along its natural path... when you feel the need to guide your stomach's contents downward along their natural course, all you have to do is press the button on the remote in your hand.

During the hypnosis, we practiced pressing the button several times. We emphasized the post-hypnotic suggestions in various forms to strengthen his control over this "gate" through an imaginary button on a virtual remote.

I asked him to practice self-hypnosis three times a day, after he had trained in it in the therapy room. I explained to him the necessary conditions and the termination method. During the hypnosis, I stressed numerous suggestions indicating that mental and physical relaxation results from a loosening that can be achieved through three deep breaths, since the expansion of the stomach depends on his relaxation and his inner calm (here, expansion is both an emotion of well-being and an action denoting enlargement. It is important to note that in hypnotic states, due to the bypassing or weakening of intellectual control mechanisms, thought reverts to a primitive and tangible level, and words are understood in their literal sense.) The flow moves only forward, and for extra assurance, there is that same button which allows him, by pressing it, to push the food forward and transfer it to the intestines.

I focused on the "light" material he provided during that session, for he had given me two metaphors, and I chose to proceed with one of them without consulting him. "The stomach of a thirteen-year-old" (his age when his mother died), or perhaps there should be "something to prevent the food from going back up."

The question that troubled me at that moment was – what is the most important thing, from my point of view, to focus on now? Should I go back to age thirteen, the age when he lost his mother, and search for the reasons that "left" his stomach as it is, without developing and growing as he matured, or should I postpone that subject and begin with the metaphor of "something to prevent the food from going back up"?

I decided to begin with the latter.

Of course, if the therapy were to continue over time, there was the possibility of addressing that trauma which, for some reason, had left his stomach "stuck" at this early stage of his life.

I also thought there was no need to deal with "things the stomach fails to digest, which then come back out." I mentioned that issue to him during the hypnosis only, leaving any further discussion of it to his subconscious.

Personally, I don't know what happened between the sessions. Nor do I fully know what transpired during the sessions themselves. I guided him to the "safe place" he told me about in our first meeting, and from there I worked with him—or with his subconscious to address his problem.

After three sessions of hypnosis treatment, I asked him:

"How are you feeling today, Adel?"

"Two out of ten," he replied with a smile.

Earlier, we had established a scale of ten levels, where the highest level signified a dire assessment of the situation, and the lowest represented a normal state or the desired goal. At the start of the treatment, Adel was at level nine, and now he has reached level two, with the goal being level one.

During the past two weeks, he took a Dramamine pill only once, after having taken these pills nearly every day. He vomited only once, and according to him—as he told me—that is a great success.

And the surprise – he is in love with one of his female colleagues, and they agreed to meet immediately after our last session.

He paid for three sessions, said goodbye to me, and left the clinic.

' ' '

By chance, I ran into him at one of the malls, his arm intertwined with that of a girl.

"Hello, Doctor," he said.

"Hey there, Doctor," I replied.

He smiled, and I smiled, and after he had walked away, my wife whispered to me:

"Look at how a man should walk with his beloved."

She neither asked anything nor showed any interest...

She only remarked with a smile: "Learn from the doctor!"

And she linked her arm with mine.

Chapter 12

Dr. Ayman

Fear of illnesses and death

He did not understand how he ended up at the hospital that day.

All he remembered from that evening was the pain that suddenly struck his chest, the sound of the ambulance siren that carried him to the hospital, and the snow that fell quietly outside.

He had never liked the sound of the ambulance siren, yet he did not hate it either. At least, that's what he told me when we met. He said his attitude toward it was neutral, and he often didn't even notice it when the ambulance passed by. Perhaps he chose to ignore it, for he did not want to acknowledge that within it lay someone teetering between life and death, lying there unwillingly on a stretcher. At the same time, one of the paramedics watched over him and treated him with an injection of adrenaline, an oxygen mask, or a series of electric shocks to revive his heart, exhausted from life's struggles. And perhaps he did not wish to be troubled by the thought that inside him someone was suffering at that very moment, whose life depended on how quickly he reached the hospital, on the mood of the drivers on the road, on the maturity of their "self," on the way they thought and how much they understood and accommodated the other.

It is known to everyone unfortunate enough to come near a driver who, in his peripheral vision, notices humiliation.

And perhaps his stance was not truly neutral as he claimed, but rather his heart harbored a deep hatred for the ambulance, since it reminded him of death more than of life.

After all, his father died in an ambulance twenty-seven years earlier, when he was thirteen, and neither the siren nor the paramedic nor the electric shocks to his bare chest had helped him.

In contrast, he loved the snow very much. When he walked alone in the evenings, he relished feeling the warmth of his body while the snow fell like feathers on his face and hair, turning them white. He adored the freshness and purity that came to cover the earth and dress the streets in new garments, free from any trauma or suffering. And perhaps for that reason, he wished for his hair to whiten prematurely. They say that old age is an honor, and he believed that in old age there is wisdom and beauty. The snow bestowed those sensations upon him, if only for a few moments, and he sought something — anything else — to distract him from himself.

Such was the magnitude of his self-repudiation!

When his gaze was fixed, he saw nothing except those moments when he walked behind the coffin, where his father's body lay.

All he remembered was that he cried, stomped his feet on the ground, and that he called for his father to wake up.

It is not that he didn't understand what death is. His understanding was sufficient to grasp that there is no return from death. He learned this in school when one of his classmates died from a severe illness. His chair remained empty throughout the year; no one sat in it, and his friend never returned.

He refused to believe that his father's chair in the family divan (the entertaining quarters) would also remain empty, due to the psychological defense mechanisms that served to protect the soul from the terror of that trauma.

When I see and hear him, I recall those moments at my own father's funeral when people followed his coffin. I was five years old then. I don't remember exactly what caused me to leave the gathering, the shouting and crying. Still, instead, I went to the neighbors' house on the second floor to play on the balcony overlooking the street where the funeral procession passed. I watched the people from above and continued playing without any significant emotion, without giving the event any special attention as if it were just another occurrence.

I did not shout, nor did I ask my father, who lay in the coffin, to wake up.

They told me that my father was dead. I saw a crowd of people and heard them crying. Darkness covered my eyes, and I fell silent. I said nothing and revealed none of my inner feelings. I left the house quietly and went to play with the neighborhood children as I did every day.

I did not cry, of course.

I knew that my father was dead and that he would no

longer take me with him to the madafa (the family guest wing), where he used to bring me along occasionally. He would no longer tell me that I was a smart child and that one day I would be a school principal.

I felt the stares of my classmates fixed on me, expressing a little pity and a lot of derision, and I understood that from that day onward I would bear the title of "orphan."

It was a "shame" or a "curse" that I carried for years, through no fault of my own.

My father died when he was forty.

A few months after I celebrated my fortieth birthday, I found myself on a bed in the cardiac unit of a hospital, following a disruption in that magical melody emanating from the heart, which did not return to its normal rhythm except by means of electric shocks, not in the natural way.

Let us return to our friend. Every time February arrived and snow began to fall, he would walk at night to the boardwalk near his home, strolling for his own pleasure and delighting in the gently falling snow, which served as a cover for the cypress trees and cloaked the ground in a brilliant, sparkling layer reminiscent of pearls thanks to the lights emanating from the old power poles above them.

He loved February's snow; it would transport him back to his childhood days when he was often fortunate enough to enjoy the warmth of his mother's bed on cold winter nights.

But today, he had begun to hate what he once regarded with neutrality.

He began to despise the things he had loved about February and all that he had cherished since childhood.

He started to loathe the resonant sounds, the snow, the color white, and the month of February.

Actually, no—perhaps "hate" is not the precise word. In public, he used that term, yet privately, the word that truly expressed his feeling was "fear."

Indeed, he began to fear all of these. He started to fear the month of February and everything associated with it.

His list of fears grew longer and gradually came to dominate his worries, paralyzing him and disrupting his life.

In short, he began to fear death.

That evening, he sat alone by his writing desk, which was strewn with various books and summaries of several important lectures. The glow of the open computer screen was reflected in his glasses, and the light from the desk lamp added to their brilliance. Outside, it was cold, and the snow continued unabated. He heard in the news report that this weather was expected to persist throughout the weekend.

Such weather typically characterizes the beginning of February, and he did not expect it now with the approach of March.

The snow had accumulated on the window of the room on the ninth floor of a sixteen-story building, and on the windowsill rested a basket of nonperishable food that included meats, a few slices of salmon fillet, and some frozen vegetables. The snow had draped it with a white mantle, a sign that the season for using the room's refrigerator had yet to arrive.

And that's not all.

The force of the snowstorm had seeped through the double-glazed window and reached his ears, and despite his solitude, it brought him great pleasure or at least so it appeared to him. I cast this doubt; that is my addition.

I express doubt about that, for I believe that if he had truly been enjoying himself, nothing like what happened would have occurred.

And perhaps he did indeed enjoy it...

It was nearly midnight, or just before, when suddenly he felt a stabbing in his chest followed by an involuntary movement of his hand that grazed the spot of pain and sought something as sharp as a knife destined to pierce him from a far-off place, from a distant past and a difficult childhood.

Yet he never succeeded in extracting that destructive instrument which had assailed him from his chest. He felt his heart pounding rapidly—as if, in a moment, it would burst free from its confines—and pain spread through the upper part of his abdomen. He experienced numbness in his left hand and shoulder, and sweat streamed down his face and body.

He felt as though the air within him was disappearing and that no fresh air could enter his lungs. He sensed pressure on his chest as if a large rock had taken up residence there without permission.

He had never experienced such sensations, and it occurred to him that his heart would surely stop soon, that he would die without ever finishing his studies.

"To hell with studying," he told himself. "But who will warm his mother's bed after he dies?" That thought tormented him in those moments.

It was odd that he would think so while still in the prime of life.

He began to feel as though he were suffocating, and the rhythm of his heartbeat quickened. He felt his heart shattering his ribs, desperate to break free from his weary body laden with relentless thoughts and misery.

Surely I will die... I will die now... Perhaps my lifeless body will only be discovered after a few days, once the stench of decay reaches the nostrils of Angelica, my neighbor.

These thoughts terrified him, and sweat poured off him more and more. He felt his mouth grow dry, the room spun around him, the wardrobe overturned, and the ceiling and floor seemed to have exchanged places.

And the door? He no longer knew on which side of the room it was located.

He didn't even know how to call for help, yet he found within himself a strange strength that propelled him into the hallway, and he knocked on the door of his neighbor's room, of whom all he knew was that her name was Angelica. Fortunately, she was awake at that moment.

It had been about three months ago, in the late winter season, precisely on the last day of February.

He arrived at my place dressed in a fine leather coat, a white shirt, tight jeans, and brown boots with wooden heels that clicked quietly with each step along the long corridor leading to the treatment room – tick... tick... tick...—in an effort to assert his presence and self-confidence.

His head was shaved, and his beard was black, short, and meticulously groomed. His body was that of an athlete, and despite his spring attire, his chiseled muscles were on full display. He looked neat and well-cared-for, always maintaining an elegant appearance. Yet none of this concealed the weary lines of his face, his red, sorrowful eyes, and the forced smile he managed to display between words that only added to his pain.

A few days earlier, he had celebrated his fortieth birthday with childhood friends who had surprised him while he was alone in his small room.

He is married to Salma, who works as a kindergarten teacher, and they have three sons — the eldest is ten and the youngest five. He was enrolled in a Ph.D. program in the social sciences at a university in Denmark, and this was his fourth and final year. He had only a few months left to fulfill his requirements and obtain his doctorate.

However, a month ago, he left it all behind and returned to his country.

He doesn't want a doctorate, no certificate, nor any further studies.

All he wants is to overcome death. He fears the moment when one of his little sons will strike the coffin in which he lies and call him to awaken and return.

If only he were certain that the dead neither hear, nor understand, nor see, nor feel anything, it might have been easier for him. Perhaps. But he does not know, and what a terrible catastrophe it would be if he died and it turned out that he could hear his sons' cries and see their tears.

It would be a second death.

He is afraid to die one death rather than to experience a second death.

But he also cannot live!

That same evening, he entered the operating room to undergo an urgent catheterization after a blockage was discovered in his coronary artery. No one was waiting for him, for he was alone in that cold northern land, in terms of both people and weather. His personality did not lend itself to easily forming social connections, and I'm not even referring here to being introverted. That is not the point. He loved his social bonds, enjoyed engaging in conversation, delighted in listening to others, and took even greater pleasure when others listened to him during social gatherings.

However, he chose his friends with extra care. In fact, they had to prove the sincerity of their connection with him before he would open his door to them. And in that country, no one is inclined to make the effort to prove the genuineness of their intentions.

He spent two days in the hospital and was discharged with a basket of various medications: a drug to balance cholesterol levels and blood pressure, beta blockers to help slow his heartbeat, and Coumadin, an anticoagulant. It is well known that this medicine thins the blood, so one must maintain a specific diet and have blood tests every two days to monitor the blood's clotting levels, as it must not exceed a certain threshold. In addition to these medications, he was advised to engage in light aerobic exercise for an hour each day.

He left the hospital in good health, yet with psychological trauma.

Since that day, the dark thoughts have never let him go. At night, he would wake from sleep repeatedly, and sometimes he wouldn't sleep at all, for fear that the night's slumber might turn into eternal sleep. He counted the days until death, convinced he wouldn't live any longer than his father, who had died at a similar age from a sudden heart attack that overwhelmed him while he was in an ambulance.

"But you prevailed over the ambulance. You arrived at the hospital alive, and here you are," I said firmly.

He looked at me in astonishment, as if surprised by my remark on his claim of having conquered death in the ambulance, unlike what happened to his father.

"You are here now," I said again, "in full physical strength, with open arteries through which blood flows to every cell of your body."

His life had completely changed. He was afraid to stray from home, and if he did venture out, it would be only in the company of one of those "saving" friends who had rushed to his aid when his heart had ceased to beat. He did not return to his studies, and the thought of them no longer occupied him. Most of the time, he isolated himself, ready and poised to confront death in order to overcome it. It was the desire of his heart, though he found it hard to believe himself.

He would undoubtedly die at some point in the future,

like every person on earth, but not now. If only he could delay his death for a few more years until his children came of age. That was his sole concern, for he knew all too well the pain of losing a father as a small child, and he would not wish that on anyone, least of all on his own children.

He wants to live for his children, yet he is afraid of death, which looms over him.

His life had changed, and thoughts of death clung to him everywhere and never let go. Would his death be sudden, or would it be a death that he would invite? A whirlwind of thoughts swirled in his mind, and fear, depression, and despair gripped him.

He had been in that state for two full months.

He had lost his appetite and become gaunt. His eyes were red, his eyelids swollen and protruding on a face that no longer reflected his youthful age.

"Strange... that power you have," I murmured to myself in a tone that reached his ears.

"I don't understand," he replied hastily in a critical tone, "what power?"

"I think... It's odd how that power you possess is invested elsewhere, in another realm, not in what you truly wish to invest it in, and not for the reason you came to me. This state of despair and depression you're in demands strength to carry on, and you need to conserve your energy, yet you squander it. For the past two months, you have been plagued almost constantly by these recent thoughts, immersing yourself in them without pause. This condition requires determination... perseverance... strength... energy. All of these, as I understand it, abound within you."

"What power are you talking about? I have lost everything... my whole life has changed... I abandoned my doctoral studies at the final stage... I can't sleep... I don't know what happened to me or why, and a million questions are racing through my head every moment... and you're talking to me about power?"

That is precisely the power he could not perceive because of a mental barrier governing his thoughts and impeding the pathways to logical reasoning, preventing even the slightest reframing or positive thinking.

"Alright," I said.

I asked him if he was willing to be hypnotized, and he responded affirmatively, although his readiness for hypnosis painted a different picture. He was one of those patients who are difficult to hypnotize.

In this case, the traditional methods of hypnosis are not effective.

So I used stories:

"You know what? I just remembered something that happened to me a few days ago. I was driving my car on the way to the clinic—well, here—and I saw a medium-sized cat sleeping in the middle of the road. The cars coming from both directions swerved aside to avoid hitting it...and yet it continued to sleep in the middle of the road. I wondered what had caused this cat to sleep there, and what I could do... I decided to stop and help it or rescue it... for if I didn't, I told myself, one of the cars would surely run it over, and it would die... I pulled my car over to the side of the road and tried to reach it. The drivers began honking to warn me and to ask me to get off the road. One car—a black car—was speeding, and had I not been careful, it would have run me over... Some drivers waved their hands or honked greetings at me once they recognized who I was. Some pulled over to let me pass, while others seemed utterly indifferent—neither to me nor to the cat lying there as good as dead in the middle of the road. Finally, I reached the cat and looked at it closely. It was skinny and dirty, with a bleeding swelling on its face that distorted one of its eyes, perhaps as a result of a violent fight with another cat over territory or over the favors of a nearby female, or perhaps due to illness or some other cause rooted in the garbage bins where most cats spend their time. As is my daily habit, I had put on my new, shiny shoes — important to me — and at that moment I was wearing beige trousers. Truthfully, I did not want to touch the cat with my hands to move it, for I feared I might catch some contagious disease or get dirty; I was also worried about small insects that were likely infesting its filthy fur, an ideal environment for life, pleasure, and breeding... So I used my feet softly and cautiously so as not to add to the cat's suffering, and I tried to move it from the middle of the road... And what were the cars doing at that very moment? Several curious drivers slowed down to observe what was happening... Other drivers warned me and called out for me to leave the cat to its fate, for its destiny was clearly to be run over. "Doctor, you'd be wise to let it be," they advised... and some drivers even mocked, laughed, and jeered repeatedly... I did not listen to what they said, and since I love pets and used to keep cats in my apartment at the student dorms during my psychology studies, my compassion for the cat overwhelmed me. Yet every time I moved it, it returned to the middle of the road and fell asleep. I moved it once, twice, even a third time—and each time it hurried back to its spot, as if a magnet were drawing it back..."

"Leave it, man... leave it, Doctor," most of the drivers who had taken an interest in the scene told me.

The cat's behavior struck me as marvelous. It possessed an extraordinary courage, remarkable strength, and a fierce determination to remain in that dangerous spot. It was not afraid of either the cars or me, and every time it returned to its place in the middle of the road—a road crossed by dozens of cars every minute.

It had determination, courage, and astonishing strength.

Finally, after it had overcome me, I left it, returned to my car, and continued on my way here.

When I got into the car, I remembered another incident that happened to me about a year or so ago. That one, too, involved a cat. One morning, I saw in my yard a cat missing a hind leg — a cat with three legs.

My wife and I pitied it... poor thing... How can a three-legged cat live alone and provide for itself? In our neighborhood, on one of the city's outskirts, most cats love to hunt mice, birds, and reptiles — simply because our garbage bins contain little trash, as there are few houses and no restaurants, shops, or banquet halls that dump their refuse into the local bins.

Anyway, we decided to adopt that cat and feed it.

To our great surprise, it never once approached the bowl of food we had prepared for it. Nor did it come near us. It was always in the yard, and many times I would see it among the citrus trees, especially beneath the orange tree.

From then on, I began to notice in the early hours of the morning feathers drifting here and there and the remains of dead birds and reptiles — among them a large, intact black scorpion that I found on the doorstep that morning. I was convinced that the one responsible for all this was the three-legged cat. I figured it had torn its prey apart at night and left the remnants in the yard. I have no idea what the cat meant by leaving those remains so near the doorway... after all, it is disabled and should be nearing the end of its life, unless someone helps it and feeds it each day. But it decided to live despite its condition, and even insisted on being a whole cat despite its disability. It decided to live, come what may!

In fact, I did not know whether that cat was male or female, for I was interested only in its condition, and I hadn't noticed the triangular shape of its small head that would have revealed it to be a female, since male cats have larger heads.

After about two months or so, I saw that disabled cat again, whom we had nicknamed in the family Umm al-Tal'at Argul (the three-legged one), trailing behind her four kittens that quickly clung to her belly in search of teats from which to suck a little milk.

This cat was so wonderful—her strength was extraordinary, and her refusal to accept the help we tried to offer was just as remarkable. Perhaps she was trying to tell us something...

Where does she get that strength? I wondered—not only did she refuse to give in, but she also insisted on giving birth.

All four of her kittens grew up—each with four legs—and my children decided to adopt one of them, which remains with us to this day.

By the way, the cat returns to us from time to time, accompanied by one or two kittens, and she is still out there — hunting, mating, and giving birth.

And she is three-legged.

How marvelous are the powers of this cat, and the extent of her determination!

There are all kinds of cats... Some get injured in the face and decide to lounge in dangerous spots amid fast-moving cars, while others—a disabled three-legged cat, for instance —choose to continue living, opting for life as they keep sleeping among the citrus trees and hunting birds and reptiles.

The truth is, I will never know what became of that cat in the middle of the road... perhaps one of the cars ran it over... maybe it died... I don't know... What I do know is that it chose to be there... while it is clear that this she-cat continues to live, giving birth to more kittens and investing her strength and energy... in the name of life. That was her choice."

I finished telling him my story and fell silent. He sat in his chair, listening with full attention until the end, and even appeared relaxed and at ease after entering a light hypnotic trance. For clarification, it is customary to use stories as an effective tool to accelerate hypnotic induction (the initial part of the hypnosis process, the preliminary stage necessary to enter a hypnotic state).

It was during the second meeting—which lasted a bit longer than scheduled—that he stood up, shook my hand, and said, "Thank you... Thank you." Then he left the room without looking back. He did not schedule another appointment and said he would call me if needed. Just a week later, he sent me a message in the same tone: "I loved that three-legged one..."

After three months, I received a telephone invitation

from him to visit Copenhagen, to participate in the degree conferral ceremony scheduled for this coming September.

"Make a note in your calendar, Doctor... Bring along your wife and children, my treat.

'The three-legged one' will manage just fine without you..." he said.[9]

Chapter 13

Aboudi

Insomnia

It is now midnight, or a little after midnight. In the neighborhood and throughout the city, a quiet calm prevails, occasionally broken by the soft, hazy rustling of the nearby trees' leaves swaying in the gentle breezes.

It had been an hour since he went to bed, and he was sleeping a quiet, deep sleep.

Suddenly, he began to breathe rapidly. He inhaled, and before the air could reach his lungs, he exhaled it and drew in another breath.

Inhale and exhale...

Half an inhalation and half an exhalation...

Inha... exha...

In... ex...

He felt as though he was being suffocated, and a direct command came from his inner brain—the limbic system, which is responsible for the involuntary functions common to all living beings, such as breathing, blood pressure, and heart rate, as well as for emotions and wakefulness and sleep:

"Get up! There is danger!"

He leapt out of bed, letting out an unintelligible scream, placing his hand on his neck and groping it in search of something tightly wrapped around it to choke him — perhaps a rope or a pair of unfamiliar hands poised to do him in. "The amygdala" is the small part of his brain's limbic system that protects him from threats; it suddenly awakened and began performing its duty at a pace he did not expect. The level of cortisol — the hormone famously known as the "stress hormone," essential for survival and one that has safeguarded mankind through its struggles throughout history — began to rise. His heart rate quickened, and he was drenched in sweat. Thanks to that amygdala, he rapidly prepared for an impending attack or escape. His body and all its systems entered into a confrontation that seemed very real, and he felt a suffocating fear and anxiety, as though betrayed by a stray bullet—or by any other unforeseen calamity.

But he found neither a rope nor any unfamiliar hands.

He didn't even hear any gunshots in the air at that moment.

Gunshots from unlawful firearms, which, in the absence of law enforcement and authority, have become part of the natural acoustic environment in Arab community settlements over the past two decades.

He found nothing.

Everything was in its place — the glass of water on the nightstand by the bed, the alarm clock beside it, two mathematics textbooks, and many notebooks scattered on a new desk his father had bought him ahead of his high school matriculation exams.

He slept in his room, enjoying a privilege that set him apart from his three sisters, who shared the second room. Pale light seeped in from the hallway, while darkness reigned in his parents' bedroom.

Thank God, no one was awakened by his scream.

He sipped a little water from the glass he always kept by his side each night in case he felt thirsty, calmed down a bit, took a deep breath in the hope that the air would sustain him until morning, sighed quietly, and went back to sleep.

Sometimes he does not remember what happened during the night, nor does he feel a thing. He wakes up with screams, gropes his neck, wipes away the sweat that has soaked him, calms down, and falls back asleep.

Other times, he feels the dampness on the bed and is embarrassed by himself, much more so when his mother spreads his mattress along the fence that divides their house from the neighbors'.

In the morning, he wakes up with difficulty, his face creased and his mood sullen, after several shouts from his mother and sisters urging him to get up and demanding that he turn off the alarm clock, whose sound continues to echo throughout the small house.

"Aboudi, for God's sake, turn off the clock... Oh, woe to you, get up already!"

This call has been repeated every morning since he began high school three years ago. However, its sharpness and frequency have only grown over the last year—especially during the period when he was preparing for his matriculation exams and the psychometric test.

Every morning, he would get to school exhausted. At times, he would merely change his underwear, for he never found time to shower. When he arrived at school, the scent of dried urine clinging to his body would waft around him, and he would distance himself from his friends. If only he could, he would even distance himself from his very self so as not to smell the odor of his soul.

Salma, his eldest sister, began her pediatric residency this year at the nearby hospital after completing her studies at one of the universities in Germany.

Salwa, his middle sister, is finishing her studies in architecture here this year.

And Samira, his youngest sister, began her studies this year for a bachelor's degree in English literature.

Abdul Islam, or in short Abd, preferred to be addressed by his childhood affectionate nickname, Aboudi. He was the youngest in the family. He was born about a month earlier than expected, and so the doctors had to keep him in the hospital for a few extra days for observation.

In his childhood, he was terribly spoiled as the youngest one and the "heir", apparently destined to carry on the family line and preserve its honor. And, by the way, it wasn't that the family denied his sisters any pampering, but his share far exceeded theirs combined.

In elementary school, he faced various difficulties, especially suffering from attention deficit and hyperactivity. Yet the care of his parents and the concern of his sisters helped him overcome many hurdles.

His grades were generally mediocre, but he constantly heard his parents whispering to each other, saying "he's retarded" and that "nothing will ever come out of him." Yet openly they expressed their desire to send him to study at that same German university where his older sister had studied.

Deep in his heart, he knew he wasn't cut out for such studies and that he would most likely finish the 12th grade with such limited success that it wouldn't allow him to be admitted to any university at all.

Fifteen years had passed since the day when Aboudi awoke for the first time, terrified, feeling that he was suffocating.

His involuntary nocturnal urination finally ceased, but the episodes of nighttime anxiety returned and recurred. Initially, they only woke up his parents, but later they began to disturb the rest of the family. During those years, each of his sisters began to pursue her field of specialization, then got married, started a new family, and left home.

Aboudi also got married, and two years ago, a delightful baby was born to him, whom he named Amal (Hope). He continued to live in the family home, sharing it with his parents.

He presented his former room to his son after making several changes to it: he painted its walls in shades of blue and hung several paintings and photographs of children on them.

The anxiety attacks persisted, but now his wife had taken it upon herself to care for him.

During these years, Aboudi underwent a lengthy series of various medical tests, including assessments in a sleep laboratory as well as examinations of brain waves, eye movements, the diaphragm, breathing, lung function, leg motions during sleep, heart function, blood pressure, and oxygen levels, among other tests. None of these revealed anything that could explain his condition or that required any particular medical intervention.

An MRI (magnetic resonance imaging) scan of the brain was also performed.

"There is no finding necessitating medical treatment," was always the result, a fact that further heightened the tension and anxiety of Aboudi and his parents.

"If only we knew what the cause was, then we wouldn't be groping in the dark and we would be treating the problem."

That was what everyone had hoped for.

But the same was said about the issue of nocturnal enuresis, which vanished in tandem with the onset of sleep problems.

No cause or explanation was found for the bedwetting, despite the many tests conducted on him. A pediatric specialist in enuresis (the medical term for involuntary nocturnal urination) referred him to psychological treatment after performing a series of tests and administering various medications aimed at slowing urine production during the night, in addition to drugs to soothe the bladder, reduce its contractions, and increase its capacity.

Incidentally, this is what typically happens with patients for whom traditional medicine fails to find an appropriate treatment; then psychiatry or psychological therapy becomes their recourse.

Despite everything, this nighttime anxiety had become part of the parents' daily routine, and his wife was also drawn into this whirlwind.

The father would wake from his slumber, ask what was wrong, and then go back to sleep.

The mother would awaken from her sleep, bring him another glass of water, and then go back to sleep.

And now that responsibility has transferred to the wife. She awakens from her sleep, soothes her husband, and attempts to return to sleep.

Everything was proceeding "naturally" until the event that set off a red warning light for them occurred.

The son, Amal, joined this routine without consulting anyone. He began to wake in anxiety from his father's shouting and was unable to fall back asleep.

At a social event, I happened to encounter his father by chance. I had a rather casual connection with him in the past, which had been severed due to the age gap between us, him being several years older than me, and also because of our different professional interests.

He shared his stories with me, and I saw his eyes gleaming with happiness as he spoke of his daughters' achievements.

"And how is Aboudi?" I asked.

The last time I saw Aboudi was when I went to study in Moscow. He was three years old at the time. Since then, I had not seen him, and had I encountered him now, I certainly wouldn't have recognized him.

At my inquiry, he suddenly fell silent, and his body language clearly indicated that he was in distress. He looked away, perhaps out of embarrassment—or perhaps out of caution in case someone might overhear him—and said:

"For God's sake, I don't know what to say to you... that child worries me and the entire family."

He continued, explaining to me in a low voice and in painstaking detail how he woke in anxiety and worry, and was unable to help his son, and how all the tests had shown no significant findings. Then he fixed his gaze on me, and, quite suddenly, his demeanor changed. He moved closer, as if he wanted to shout "Eureka!" (I've found it!) like Archimedes when he ran out of his house naked and declared:

"You can surely help him! I've heard that you practice hypnosis, and I'm confident that hypnosis will help that child."

In truth, the father voiced exactly what I had been thinking at that moment: the child needed hypnosis to sleep.

However, all this took place during a brief, impromptu conversation at a fleeting social gathering between two people who once shared a friendly connection, whereas now the objective is to give the dialogue a professional and official character, to transition it from the street into the clinic.

And as we all know, this is a fundamental condition for the success of therapy. Moreover, therein lies the challenge we face: we, the Arab experts, who live and work professionally in a well-known social environment—where we all take part in various social events, walk its streets every day, enter its shops, share its intimate atmosphere and limited space, and experience firsthand the events unfolding within it.

How can you maintain professionalism, for instance, if you suddenly encounter your patient while he's giving you a piece of his mind behind a fruit stand at the market? Or when you're buying vegetables from a vendor who, as you pay him, asks, how can his son's problem at school be solved. Or when a bank clerk asks you for advice on how to resolve his issue with his wife? Or when a man sitting next to you at a funeral home says, "All your psychological methods are worthless... today's generation only understands beatings"?

Will you respond with silent agreement?

Will you engage in an argument, knowing that under normal circumstances it would go on for hours and never end?

Will you tell him that it is his opinion — which you respect — yet you oppose it?

Or perhaps you will ignore him as if you hadn't heard him, and speak with him about another subject, such as the weather or the late hour, or inquire about details you already know, such as the deceased's age, the reason for his death, and so forth...

The middle ground and the quest for balance between personal knowledge and experience and the clinical encounter is a task that I believe we professionals understand: on one hand, we recognize its risks and inherent limitations, and on the other, its importance and the advantages it offers at a professional and therapeutic level.

Already the next day, Aboudi called me after obtaining my business card, which I had given to his father during our conversation without any explicit purpose. He called to set up a therapeutic appointment, after having confirmed that I am, indeed, a hypnosis expert.

A tall, slender young man entered the clinic; he had a long, prominent nose and tired eyes, deeply sunken in their sockets and barely visible.

"What's your story?" I asked him.

The way I opened the session surprised him, and after a few moments of silence, during which he seemed to ponder what to say or how to begin, he said:

"I think a lot about... I could have done well in my studies, but in high school, there was a significant decline in my grades. I often wonder why it happened to me, and I deeply regret not having listened to my parents."

"I hear you telling me that if you had listened to your parents, your situation would have been different."

"Not exactly... actually, perhaps yes, indeed... but my father was very irritable. I tried, for example, to learn his trade and become a carpenter like him... I love carpentry... but I simply couldn't work with him. Today I work with my uncle, who is also a carpenter."

"You want to be a carpenter... like your father, even if you learn the trade from someone else."

"Yes, I can be a good carpenter. The fact is that today I manage all the orders at my uncle's carpentry shop."

"You've proven that the vocation is tailor-made for you!"

"My father always told me, when I worked with him, that I would amount to nothing, and he would get angry with me over every little thing."

"I understand from you that you are connecting these issues you've described to the sleep problems you told me about on the phone."

"I don't know... maybe..."

"Hold on, help me understand what the reason is that you sought me out."

"I haven't been sleeping, doctor... for a long time now... and the problem is that my son has begun to wake up from my yelling... I simply can't stand my situation anymore."

"I understand. Tell me about the place where you feel you can sleep peacefully... a place where you feel calm and secure."

Here, through suggestion, I implanted in him the idea that there exists a safe place where he can sleep undisturbed, and he merely had to define it for me. The safe place is one of the tools we utilize during therapy, and this is the second reason for my request.

"In the north... in the Golan Heights... more precisely, at the Hatzbani Stream."

He continued and described the Hatzbani Stream to me, and that particular safe place where he feels he can sleep in peace.

After I finished gathering information about his condition and collecting the critical details for the therapy, and after assessing his suitability for hypnosis, we commenced the treatment.

It was clear to me that there was a need to act on several levels, since behavioral treatment through hypnosis yields a rapid result that serves to boost his self-esteem and therapeutic motivation. Additionally, it would allow me to help him unlock the closed chambers of his heart and engage in an inner dialogue about his relationship with his father, as well as understand the link between his self-expression and his expression of fears, and the continuity of his sleep and the nature of his dreams.

"The Hatzbani... green trees soaring... their tops dancing with the gusts of wind... the branches of the maple, oak, and eucalyptus trees, usually scattered in the area, arch over and cast shade on the water quietly flowing... the chirping of birds here and there and the sound of water gently streaming without pause among the many, round, slippery stones. Smooth rocks on both sides of the river guard its waters to prevent them from spilling over, giving it a sense of security in this place. The pleasant scent of the water and the trees reaches your nostrils without asking permission... the time – late afternoon. Sunrays pierce through the gaps between the densely packed branches and leaves, casting a pleasant, soft light upon the water and both banks of the river... You sit on a large, smooth stone... dipping your feet into the water... You feel their pleasant coolness... You sit alone... a few meters away, your wife lies on the ground and beside her, your son sleeps on a mat... He accompanied you on your journeys everywhere... your son is immersed in deep sleep after having eaten lunch... you watch the water flow, overwhelming everything in its path... it flows quietly... and just as it flows with power, with strength, and quietly, so does your son sleep... both flow... both grant themselves the joy of the flow... your son in sleep and the water in its very flow... and you... you... as you now flow in focus, in thought, and in your imagination... and as you now flow calmly and securely... perhaps you will be surprised at the flow of your sleep tonight... and tomorrow... and the night after... and whenever you wish... perhaps you will be surprised at the flow of sleep within you... a deep, flowing, and calm sleep... a strong sleep... that always finds its way among the rocks... just as the water now flows in complete tranquility, so too does your sleep... calm... serene... continuous... pleasant... pure... flowing quietly... securely... penetrating everything... flowing quietly... securely... powerfully... reaching every place you desire... everything before it is possible... every plan... idea... opinion... feeling... emotion... is expressed with absolute confidence and boldness... water and sleep and a river and day and a bed and a night... quiet and sound, darkness and the pleasure of the flow... in the continuity of sleep... the deep sleep and the deep river... just as the river flows, so too does your sleep... deep... continuous... flowing... calm..."

For about twenty minutes, Aboudi (Abdul Islam) was in a state of hypnosis. His body and the muscles of his face appeared relaxed, and his breathing was slow and serene.

I began counting backwards from ten to one, accompanied by the suggestion that with each number he hears, he would begin to return to his natural state and recall what is beneficial for him and his condition.

At one, he opened his eyes, and a slight smile appeared on his face. He asked me how long he had been in that state.

One of the characteristics of hypnotic states is the absence of a sense of time. Usually, patients expect an hour or more of sleep, while the entire process lasts much less time.

In any case, it was evident that he was at ease. The suggestions I gave him during the hypnosis would accompany him throughout the week, and let's see what happens next, I told myself.

Aboudi arrived for the second session a quarter of an hour early and waited. I observed him as the previous patient left, and from his body movements, I understood that he was tense. His legs moved restlessly, and his hands were clasped tightly. I summed up the session that had just ended and, in the process, asked myself what these movements concealed and why he had arrived early.

I felt uncomfortable, not understanding the source of this feeling. Some attribute such a sensation to the professional "perfection" I always strive for. Perhaps that was the reason...

Maybe nothing has changed...

Maybe he did not benefit from the treatment...

And maybe he came to tell me that I had failed in my therapy...

"But I've only met him once, and it would be unjust to judge me based on a single session," the rational voice within me said.

Aboudi entered at the appointed time, even though I was eager to satisfy my curiosity and receive him earlier.

"Five, doctor, today I'm at level five! This week I slept well... I woke up once every two days, and rather lightly. I didn't disturb anyone. When I woke up, I immediately fell back asleep without any outbursts. My wife asked me what happened that I stopped waking up. By the way, she doesn't know that I've been coming to see you."

The tension I had seen earlier had given way to excitement and joy at the fact that he came bearing good news.

Why the hell did my interpretation take me to negative places?

A week before, he had assessed himself as being at level ten – the highest level on the scale.

Now, being in the middle, he only had four levels left to reach the goal he had set for himself – level one.

I dedicated the second session to practicing self-hypnosis and asked him to perform it twice a day.

When he came to the third session, he was at level three, even closer to his goal, and I decided that it was time to discuss ways of self-expression, especially conveying fears and opinions that are inconsistent with those of his father and his surroundings, and that do not conform to them. We worked on coping with difficult situations through hypnosis.

Aboudi left the session with tools for assertive behavior, as well as many suggestions, both direct and indirect, aimed at strengthening his self-confidence and reinforcing genuine social connections.

Was there a connection between the involuntary nocturnal wetting and the suppressed anger he felt toward his parents?

Are his sleep problems yet another facet of the anxiety linked to that anger toward his parents, especially toward his father, who refuses to pass on the carpentry trade because he does not believe in his abilities, even though he never gave him a chance to prove them?

Does the night mark the beginning of a struggle stemming from the subconscious that had proven to him that he always wins?

In any case, the answers to all these questions that raced through my mind were clear to me, and I did not ask Aboudi to confirm or deny them.

But now there is a new victim of this struggle—the son who, through no fault of his own, was born into the midst of a fierce and prolonged conflict among the adults surrounding him.

After three sessions, he asked to take a long break.

I agreed, since I enjoy hearing good news after a pause in therapy.

And indeed, that was the news after about two months.

Aboudi drifts in his sleep at night, and the same goes for his marital life and his relationships with his father and the people around him.

"Tell me, Aboudi... how are you?" I began the session.

"I'm sorry, doctor, but my name is Abd al-Islam," he said firmly, accompanied by a smile.

He discontinued the use of his childhood nickname...

His name from now on... "Abd al-Islam"!

Chapter 14

Emil

Test Anxiety

After returning from school, he ate his lunch—or rather, part of it—to quiet his hunger, and then he went into his room.

And he did not come out.

A double bed made of mahogany, topped with a luxurious king-size mattress. A writing desk on which sits a Mac computer, and beside it a new cellphone, also an Apple product, with its box still standing beside it. On the wall hang several pictures of the snow-covered Alps, a picture of Niagara Falls, and a picture of Big Ben, which was apparently taken with a high-altitude aerial camera, perhaps from the London Eye. Above the bed hangs a large picture of Red Square, in which he appears standing between his parents.

He sits in the chair by the writing desk that his father bought for him when he renewed his office furniture, preparing for a physics exam that will take place in two days.

He flips through a book and solves several problems with ease. He reads about the laws of motion and speed, about a straight line, and practices them. Everything proceeds as usual.

At 7:30 in the evening, he hears the Mercedes driving into the courtyard and the sound of the electric gate creaking shut behind it. A few moments later, he hears the front door close and the footsteps of his father.

He knows exactly what will happen in the next moments: immediately after entering the house, his father hangs the keys on a wooden board beside the door. He places the Prada bag — which he bought during a family trip to Paris — in a closet built specifically for that purpose and which holds exactly three bags. Then he takes off his Armenian coat, hangs it on the wooden rack, removes his shoes, approaches his wife, lightly kisses her on the lips, and asks about him.

He watches his father's steps from his room and waits. A few moments of silence pass. "Now they're talking about me," he tells himself. The kitchen is adjacent to his room, and he can hear the sound of dishes being loaded into the dishwasher and the clinking of glasses as they are set on the table. He can even hear his father's voice chewing his food and the sound of water boiling in the tea kettle.

"I'm fed up, woman. I don't know what to do with him."

"I don't know what else can be done. We spoke with the class teacher and the counselor and got him a private tutor, and nothing changed. I'm afraid he'll deteriorate even further."

"82 in Biology? That's a joke... 82?!"

"You're to blame. You spoiled him too much. You gave him everything he asked for."

"I don't know, woman, we only have this one child."

And so the conversation continued, with the father laying out his concerns about him to his wife. Sometimes she shared his worries and accused him of being the cause, and at other times it was an ordinary, quiet conversation as a feeling of helplessness took over them both. Neither knew the path that would lead their son to achieve excellent results as he had in middle school, when his average was a hundred percent. Now he is about to finish tenth grade, and his grades range from C to A.

From his room, he hears every whisper and every sigh. He hears the movements of his father's eyes and hears his mother smacking her head with her hand.

He closes his eyes. Now he can hear the beating of their hearts, their thoughts, their love for him, and even the depletion of their energy. He can hear their dissatisfaction with his achievements and with him. Their disappointment is especially great, as throughout their lives, they were accustomed to striving, succeeding, and fulfilling dreams.

He hears everything, even when they do not speak in his presence. He hears what they meant to say but did not.

But now he feels a profound anger and a need to punish himself.

"I'm a failure... I'm a loser... My parents deserve to be proud of me."

He puts great effort into his studies and understands the material, and he even became a leading figure among his classmates. But recently something happened to him that he had never experienced before, and he does not understand it nor know what caused it. Nevertheless, the outcome is clear —he cannot fulfill his wish for "my parents to be proud of me" and cannot realize their dream of his success. And perhaps he will not be able to choose a path that will lead him to a respectable profession in the future—medicine like his mother, or law like his father.

Over the past few months, he listened to many "lectures" and knew them by heart. He even remembered the sequence of their sentences. The "lecture" begins in a calm tone and measured language: "We gave you everything; we spared nothing for you." "What are you lacking, my dear?" and later: "Tell me, what do you want? We are ready to give you everything you want — as long as you study and do us honor. Listen to the people around you, listen to your teachers. You must understand that your future depends on your academic achievements and your grades. Tomorrow you will find yourself on the street."

He bows his head and sighs, then continues to invest effort in his physics studies to prove, this time, that he is capable of meeting the expectations of his parents and people in general.

Let us go back an entire year.

His name is Emil, and he is a tenth-grade student. He goes to school to take the midterm exams. Everything is proceeding normally. All his grades are excellent as always. Today, he is taking a Biology exam, his favorite subject, which will surely become the main focus of his professional career in the future, as he aspires to be a doctor and to specialize in neurosurgery.

Some of the students in his class gather around him, asking about topics they did not understand or requesting additional explanations. Emil is the go-to person for all questions. He smiles and fills the role of the teacher, explaining as much as he can until the bell rings. Everyone enters the classroom, takes their seat one by one, and waits for the teacher to come in and distribute the exam papers. Some experience accelerated heartbeats, others flush, while some show no signs of anxiety at all. A few even eagerly await the test to discover the extent of their knowledge on the subject.

Emil usually belongs to the latter group.

But this time, his feelings betrayed him. The moment the teacher approached him and handed him the paper, a strange emotion seized him, one he had never known before. He had never been afraid of exams nor suffered from exam anxiety, yet something peculiar happened for the first time in that very moment.

He tried to ignore that feeling and began writing the exam. He cast a quick glance over the questions and noticed a term he was supposed to define, about which he knew very little. He did not finish reading all the instructions, for had he read them, he would have known that he had the option to choose a different question. All he remembered was that his heart began to pound rapidly and that he was racing toward some goal he desperately and immediately wanted to achieve.

Perhaps he was fleeing from the threat of that concept which had surprised him and might have overwhelmed him, or perhaps it was the exertion, the struggle, and the effort to reach the finish line of the exam. He did not know whether his instinct was fight or flight. The indecision between attacking the exam and overcoming it versus surrendering accompanied him throughout the test. At times he froze at the front, at other times he attacked, and sometimes he fled. As a result of the tremendous physical and mental exertion to which he was unaccustomed, he felt a dryness in his mouth, a heat spreading across his face and in his ears, and a large amount of cortisol — the infamous hormone — was secreted in his body.

His hand trembled, and he tried to delve into the reservoir of his memory, perhaps to find solutions, but he found only scant information.

He plunged deeper into his search, and the more he strained to dive, the worse his condition became. His heartbeat quickened, he was drenched in sweat, his memory weakened, and his concentration diminished.

The teacher noticed that he was struggling, hesitating, and sweating profusely, and he approached him and tried to calm him down. He did relax a bit, and after a while, he managed to write down what he could extract from his memory.

When the bell rang, all the students handed their exam papers to the teacher.

A week later, the news struck him with shock: his score was 82.

It was the first time in his life that he had received such a score. The lowest score he had received until then was 95 on a history exam, two years earlier. He asked to retake the exam, as his father instructed him, and after only a week, he took a makeup history exam and received a score of 100. But now the situation was completely different, he told himself; the grade was poor, and what was worse still was the subject of the exam, since his future studies depended on it.

And here a new path opened up before him.

A path of obtaining grades that do not match the effort invested.

A path of suffering in his relationships with family and friends, and worst of all, with himself.

His grades in most subjects had suffered and were lower compared to before; he hardly achieved an A." The meetings with the school counselor did not help him as expected.

"Perhaps you need extra time on exams, because you have learning difficulties that we are not aware of," the counselor told him.

He came to me accompanied by his mother, and she explained the problem to me – his problem, and hers and her husband's with him.

"He needs a psycho-pedagogical assessment," she said.

"Right, we need to evaluate in order to understand why he is not utilizing his abilities," I said, expressing understanding of her words while defining and clarifying the purpose of the meeting.

The heavy responsibility rests on the expert during his first meeting with those who come seeking his help. He must guide them, accompany them, help them, and provide professional advice before he attends to their requests. Often, parents come to him to have their child undergo a psychological evaluation, but they leave after a single guidance session that focuses on how to address their child's problem. Sometimes they approach him asking to treat a specific behavioral issue, yet end up receiving an intelligence test. This not only reduces material expenses and saves the parents further costs, but also helps prevent feelings of helplessness, frustration, and sometimes anger on the part of the parents, as well as the deterioration of the relationship between them and their child, when they feel that the "remedy" they requested and received from the therapist did not yield any results.

Perhaps Emil did indeed need a psycho-pedagogical assessment, since the complaints raised by him and his mother are actually related to his memory and concentration abilities. After all, there is a strong dialectical relationship — a reciprocal influence — between memory, concentration, and one's emotional state. In other words, difficulties in memory and concentration have emotional, neuropsychological, and mental causes that can lead to genuine learning difficulties, and they may very well explain Emil's condition.

One might ask: Why did this learning difficulty not appear earlier? After all, his grades in elementary and middle school were excellent.

This is an important and legitimate question, and the answer is clear. Learning difficulties can emerge at any stage in a person's life. It depends on the field in which one operates, the type of tasks performed, and, importantly, the degree of difficulty of the tasks required.

To clarify: a student may be creative at a certain stage in a subject — for instance, mathematics—and when the study materials increase and the mathematical tasks become more complex, a learning difficulty that was always there now surfaces. This can happen at any stage of studies up until entering university.

Difficulties in memory and concentration may also be related to lower intellectual abilities, but in Emil's case, all the mnemonic information he had clearly dispelled any doubt about his intellectual capacities.

It remains, then, to generally assess his memory and concentration abilities.

I gave him a simple digit-memory exercise from Wexler's intelligence tests, which also examines the ability to concentrate. When I asked him to recall a few numbers, the tension was evident on his face. He needed a great deal of support, as well as justification and legitimization for his failure, according to several explanations I had devised. In the end, he managed to achieve a score higher than the usual benchmark for this task.

From this examination, I understood that the problem was not a learning difficulty, but rather issues related to his emotional state. It is a fear of tests, or what is known as "test anxiety."

I asked him how he felt during the task he had just completed—the memory exercise.

He replied, "I was scared... I do get nervous during tests... I think I have a problem in that regard."

"What is your current level of fear regarding tests?"

"Eight out of ten," he said.

"And what is the goal you aspire to achieve?"

"Three. It's not terrible if a little fear remains, because it helps me to prepare seriously for tests."

"Three? Typically, students or patients aim for a level of zero or one—that is, a state of 'no fear at all' or only a minimal, healthy amount of fear. But Emil chose as he did, since that fear was one of his motivations and incentives to succeed. As long as this remains the case at this stage of treatment, I thought to myself, it is possible that once he achieves this goal, he will want to set another goal. Let us discuss that now.

I asked him what he knew about hypnosis, if he had ever heard anything about it, seen it by chance in a movie, or read about it. He said he hadn't heard anything at all on the subject.

After a brief explanation of hypnosis, I summarized: "When we use hypnosis, we enter unconscious pathways that bypass both control and consciousness. Then we begin to search for solutions to the psychological problems the person is facing. In addition, we can look for ways and mechanisms to reinforce a person's talents and abilities. In your case, we will look for solutions to test anxiety, alright?"

I obtained his written consent to use hypnosis, as well as his mother's consent, since he had not yet reached adulthood, and we began the treatment.

He entered a hypnotic state quickly and easily. He closed his eyes and sank into the sofa with a relaxed, heavy body. His expression was calm and relaxed; once these signs appeared, I asked him:

"Tell me, what do you see now?"

"I see stairs ascending upward... twelve stairs."

"Where are you now? On which stair?"

"I am on the tenth stair." (He is in 10th grade)

"What else do you see?"

"I see closed rooms to the right of each stair... rooms with iron doors shut."

"Aha..."

"I want to open the door to the room."

At this stage, I did not think there was a therapeutic need to open the doors of these rooms and enter them. If he sees twelve stairs and is on the tenth, perhaps the focus on continuing to climb is the goal. If any difficulty is encountered on one of the subsequent stairs, then it might become necessary to open the adjacent room to see what is concealed within.

"Good, Emil. Let's leave the room now and continue climbing. Perhaps we will return to it later and open its door. So, be calm. Do you agree?"

"I want to climb, but there is a problem on the tenth stair. I can't continue."

"Tell me... what is the problem? What is the obstacle that makes it difficult for you to continue climbing?"

"It's a gate... an iron gate... old... rusty... it is locked, and I can't open it... I also can't jump over it, because there are coils of barbed wire on it."

"I understand... I understand... There is a locked iron gate, and you can't get past it by jumping over or going around it... Look carefully around you and tell me if you can find a way to solve this problem and move past it... Something that could help you open the gate or go through it or..."

"I see the students from my class passing easily... everyone gets past it with no difficulty as if it doesn't exist... they are overtaking me... now I am alone... everyone has climbed several stairs above."

He showed signs of restlessness—his body began to tremble, his head moved quickly from side to side, and his breathing rate increased.

I explained that I needed to guide him to the safe place he had told me about earlier, so that we could continue to calmly search for a means to help him get past the gate.

"Emil, I want you to recall now that safe place you told me about... Imagine that place on the mountain, among the pine trees, in the late afternoon... the weather is warm and pleasant... gentle breezes caress the pine needles... the branches swaying in the wind create a pleasant music accompanied by the chirping of various birds... in the distance, you hear the call of a cuckoo... do you hear it? You are sitting with your friend... both of you leaning against the trunk of a pine tree... You see in the distance your parents and your friend's parents talking and laughing... You can see from afar the sea and the large ships anchored in the harbor..."

I noticed that he calmed down and that his body became relaxed, and I continued:

"Now I want you to look carefully toward the gate that is preventing you from continuing to climb the stairs upward... what do you need in order to get past it? What could help you?"

"A key," he quickly answered.

"I understand... You want to see if there is a key beside the gate... somewhere?"

"I see an old clay pot on the floor near the gate."

"Aha..."

"I see inside it a large iron key."

"What do you want to do now?"

"I want to open the gate."

And that is what he did. He opened the gate, left it open, and returned the key to its place.

Emil continued climbing stair by stair until he reached the twelfth stair—the boundary he had seen when the stairs first revealed themselves to him. Before his eyes, a vast green plain spread out with paths leading in several directions.

From where he stood, he could choose one of the routes. He felt a great joy, and a smile spread across his face as he remained in a state of deep hypnosis.

He chose one of the paths and walked it.

I asked him if he would like to open the rooms he had left behind beside the stairs.

"I don't want to go back," he said, "if I were to open the doors one after another, I wouldn't be here now."

"Very good, Emil. I wish you a successful journey."

During the instructions for emerging from hypnosis, I focused on a post-hypnotic suggestion:

"When you return to your regular life and daily studies, you will discover how great your ability is to find the key and the solution to any obstacle... alongside every obstacle there is a key that enables its removal... all you need to do is pause for a moment and imagine the safe place you told me about, then take several deep breaths and look around to find it... and you will find it. After you overcome any obstacle, you will recall the stairs that carried you upward... into a world full of opportunities and possibilities that will bring a smile to your face and grant you peace and confidence for the future."

He arrived at the next meeting with a positive report. His level of fear had dropped to level four.

I decided to focus on the next phase by encouraging, establishing, and strengthening this development.

"Tell me, Emil... your mother said you like to help in the kitchen. What do you especially love?"

"I love sweets."

"Do you like to bake cakes?"

"Absolutely... very much, especially apple pie."

After he explained how he makes apple pie with his mother, we began the hypnosis.

While he was in a state of hypnosis, additional ingredients were mixed into the apple pie he made — such as strength, self-confidence, energy, courage, and success — all blended with the flour, sugar, water, apples, and other components.

Now we had a special apple pie containing everything that Emil loves and needs to cope with his anxiety.

"Whenever you feel a kind of anxiety... of fear... during your studies, or in a test, or any other situation, just close your eyes for a few moments and take a small bite of this pie... this excellent and special apple pie... You will feel your strength grow and your self-confidence increase, and then you will draw closer to success and realize it. When you take a bite of this pie, you will feel its sweet taste giving you great strength, endless energy, and courage in your efforts to achieve your aspirations and goals."

That was the final suggestion.

Emil did not have any issues that required a psycho-pedagogical evaluation, nor did he need additional time on tests. All he needed was a reminder of the abilities inherent in him and the release of emotional blocks that had halted his energies and prevented their utilization.

Today, Emil is in his fourth year of medical studies at one of Europe's leading universities.

When I met him last summer, I asked if his pie was still sufficient for him. He smiled and said that he shares slices of it with his classmates.

Chapter 15

Rana

A nightmare or a dream

"And me?!... I am here! And what about me?! Why did you leave me?" she cried out for help in a terrified voice. She sat on the bed and continued to confront her nightmare alone while she slept.

The time was close to three in the morning.

"Don't forget me... wait for me... I am here.." she kept shouting for help. She sent desperate glances upward, lifting her head and her left hand, searching for a hand to rescue her and carry her to aloft, as if someone had flown away in haste and left her wounded and bleeding in a stormy sea full of sharks, or in the depths of a dark forest where glittering eyes and gleaming, sharp teeth lurk, waiting for the moment when they would pounce on her with carrots.

She cried out loudly and continued calling for help despite the note of despair in her voice.

She was a figure that every painter would dream of infusing with life in their painting.

He was surprised to feel the tears streaming from her eyes.

He had known her for only a few years before that. In his presence, she strove to remain as steadfast as a rock, strong and self-assured. When he began to falter, she would embrace him and clutch him to her heart, and when she sensed that her weakness was about to be exposed, she would flee from him, hurrying to her room and weeping until her tears had dried up. Afterwards, she would wipe her face, wear a gentle smile on her lips, and return to him as if nothing had happened.

She refused to be in any place where she might appear weak or anywhere that could remind her of helplessness or defeat. Every day, she would ask him if she appeared tense, and each time he would answer in the negative, which would soothe and bring a smile to her face. Her self-love and self-confidence were bolstered by hearing that firm negation, and she felt even stronger.

His desire for her to remain strong and steadfast by his side so that she could protect him did not ever stop him from telling her that he believed, "A person's strength lies chiefly in their ability to reveal their weakness.".

She smiled quietly as if saying to him, "You're dreaming, my dear, you're dreaming."

And then the dream came to her in the guise of a nightmare.

After all, there is no escaping the inevitable; if not when awake, then in sleep.

Rarely did she share her feelings with others, since she was not accustomed to revealing the depths of her heart. And perhaps it was a personal choice she made for reasons no one else could fathom. But she had traveled a long road with him, and with him she was more self-assured than ever, more open with herself than before, and loved herself more. These emotions had never arisen in her to the extent that they now did.

Yet, she still needed great assurance in order to break through and soar ever higher.

He knew all of this about her, even if she smiled quietly and said nothing.

He would "get her" from a single glance in her eyes or a brief sigh that escaped her lips.

He knew this very well.

He had never shared his feelings with anyone the way he shared them with her. He saw in her a refuge and a warm embrace — a guide and a support — and indeed, that is just what she was.

She listened to him for hours, willing to accept his opinion on everything and bestowing upon him unconditional respect, but did she shed her tears before him?

No, no!

Perhaps she stripped everything from herself, but did she strip her defense mechanisms before him? Her strength?

Never!

Now the nightmare assailed her. She spoke and cried out for help as she slept and dreamed.

Perhaps she called out to him, and he did not answer.

But he reasoned with himself, and immediately heavy feelings of guilt seized him. He approached her quietly, embraced her, kissed her on the forehead, and caressed her hair just as she had always loved. Then he placed her head back on her pillow like a small child, wiped away her tears without looking at her, and stayed with her as he drew strength and love from her, holding her hand until she calmed down and fell asleep again.

He promised himself that he saw nothing and heard nothing, for he loved her just as she wished to be seen — strong and self-assured.

The morning light rose and streamed through the gray curtains that covered the eastern side of the apartment on the fourth floor of a high-rise building.

"We fell asleep in anger, didn't we?" she asked and smiled as usual after opening her eyes.

She rested her head on his chest and began to stroke his tousled hair and his long, black beard.

"It was you who got angry before you fell asleep, not me!" he said, teasing and playful, speaking to her in his customary frank manner.

She smiled and moved on to caress the hair on his chest.

"I love you," she said, emphasizing the letter "L".

He hugged her tightly and sighed, not remembering the last time he had heard that word.

"And me?!... I'm here! And what about me?! Why did you leave me?" she cried out for help in a panicked tone. She sat on the bed and continued to confront her nightmare while in a state of hypnosis.

It was nearly half past six in the evening.

This time she wasn't alone.

She lay on the couch in the therapy room after coming to face her nightmare, which had recurred several times, immersed in hypnosis and calling for her nightmare to return so she could confront it.

He, too, was in the room at her invitation and by her wish.

"Don't forget about me... Wait for me... I'm here... I'm heeeere..." she continued to cry out for help and cast desperate glances upward.

I left her in that state for a few moments, believing that as long as that emotional reaction — the abreaction — continued, and feeling that it was fulfilling its purpose, it was better to let her be.

Sometimes we work on opening new doors and try to strengthen the emotional response, while other times, when necessary, we calm it down. And sometimes we do both at once — bolstering the emotional response to a certain degree, then calming it, then strengthening it again, and so on... This depends on the therapist's decisions, which generally spring from his professional intuition and therapeutic experience.

"Tell me what you see."

"People are flying... quickly running... they went and left me... There is a big door over there, and they emerged from it and closed it behind them... I'm running and trying to reach the door to get out... and to fly... but the door is closed... there is no key and nothing I can hold onto... The door is smooth... sticky... completely white..."

"Can you describe the place where you are? What is behind you?"

"Animals... I'm in a garden of predatory animals... all the animals are chasing me... wanting to devour me..."

Her crying gradually intensified.

"Alright... I understand that there is a group of people there who have left, fled, flown, and left you behind, exposed to predatory animals... and you have no passage to leave the path from which they emerged... I want to make sure that your imagination can find a way and deal with this situation... that your subconscious can lead you to a solution... do you want to?"

"Yes."

"What do you want to do? How do you envision the solution?"

"I want to get out of there."

"I understand. You want to get out of this garden of predatory animals."

"Ahhhh," she murmured softly, waiting for deliverance...

"If you truly want to leave this place, you only need to imagine a way out for yourself. You can stay, pound on the closed door, shout, scream for the people who left you to come back and help... just as you are doing now, or you can look for another way... what do you prefer?"

She did not respond.

"I know the decision is difficult... because you still expect them to return and open the door for you..."

"Maybe they'll have mercy on me... and come back..."

"I understand... you still expect them to return... What does your subconscious tell you? Is there another possibility?"

She did not respond.

"I am with you... I will guide you and advise you on how to utilize your inner strengths. Now you are connecting with your subconscious... for there lie all the solutions... there lie all the doors... there lie all the ways to get out... to fly... to hover... to be liberated..."

She interrupted my words and said:

"I see a hot air balloon."

"Nice... describe it."

"Its color is as blue as the sky... it has several beautiful designs on it... there are birds painted on it soaring in the sky... I am approaching it... it is on the ground... there is no one in it..."

"What do you want to do?"

"I want to get into the basket, of course."

She got into the basket and began to float. [10]

Part Three

Stories from Life

Chapter 16

I Am Nothing

Darkness... utter gloom at this hour, just after midnight.

I am driving my car along the dirt road parallel to the seashore, on my way back to my home in one of the small mountain villages on this island.

The road is empty; I relish the unknown and move forward in the intoxicating ecstasy of a conqueror rising above endless potholes along the way.

To my right, a high mountain; to my left, a slope; and below them, an expansive, dark sea— all I see ahead are the generously revealed lights of the car I'm driving.

I lower my ears to the silence, and a loud voice rises from within me:

"Stop, my dear, stop, why are you in such a hurry?"

I obey, for I listen to his inner voice.

I turn off the car's engine and lights, exit it, and lean against it. I need something to lean on, something to turn my back toward, because only then do I feel calm and secure.

There is no sound except for the silence, and no music

except for the melody of the waves reaching my ears as they dance calmly and in marvelous harmony with my breaths, my inhalations, and my exhalations.

A gentle breeze caresses my face and ears and then vanishes.

The only scent is that of the salty sea. The only sight is this moonless midnight darkness, pierced only by dim lights emerging from several distant houses and the pale glows of small fishing boats that appear and vanish, leaving you uncertain whether they come from the depths of the sea or the vastness of the sky, for the horizon that once separated them has vanished.

I lift my head toward the light, toward the skies that draw me despite my will, and I sink into my thoughts.

Countless twinkling stars abound, and the Milky Way shines in the heart of the heavens.

I lay out the path before me, lift my head once more, gaze at the stars, and imagine the distances between them. I see them like neighbors, door to door, yet I know from what I've learned that those distances up there are measured in light years.

I enter a state of hypnosis that allows me to step into the third dimension and see what exists behind and in depth.

I take a full, unrestrained breath, and immediately a question arises from within me without asking permission:

"Who are you, creature? What is your magnitude in this universe?"

"Me?! Ah... nothing... I am insignificant in the face of all I see," I reply without giving it a thought, not even for a moment.

Will this vast place in which I now find myself leave any

room for thought? Will there be room for thought when I am in such a hypnotic state?

I feel a peace spreading through my bones after my thoughts have paused, and I continue to savor the present moment —here and now— sinking deeper and deeper into this universe that draws me in.

"I am nothing," I repeat to myself.

This soothing force has an effect that no endorphins can match.

I repeat to myself once more: "I am nothing... I am nothing..."

A car rushes by, raising a cloud of dust that shatters the silence. Apparently, its driver had consumed an amount of alcohol far beyond his capacity.

I call out to him with a sympathetic tenderness, for in moments like these, my little heart can encompass an entire world:

"Stop, my dear, stop. Why are you in such a hurry? Come to me so that you may know your own magnitude."

But it seems that no sound reaches him—neither from within me nor from outside—and my compassion for him is spent.

The car vanishes quickly, like a meteor burning up in an instant.

I come back to myself and say, "I am nothing in this world."

"I am nothing... Everything I do, all my knowledge, love, and feelings—and all that I have—is fleeting.

I am nothing, even if I am a creator, even if I fight and win, or remain silent, with my heart producing no melody. My mind uttering not a word, even if I happen to remain silent in the face of an insult, and forgive, or dance drunkenly upon a dead body, or lose myself in a dance to the sounds of gunfire.

I
am
nothing!

Chapter 17

Rest in peace, Vangelis

When I discovered the sea on this island and fished for octopus, I realized that it is a tough competitor —one that even surpasses me. I admit it.

He came with his small family from a mountain village to live in a coastal village in search of a livelihood in agriculture and land work, and he established greenhouses near a mountain, in which he planted bananas, alongside watermelons and several types of vegetables.

Although he only knew how to float on water and could swim only with fins, just like me, he was always superior to me at octopus fishing.

Every time he pulled one or two octopuses from the water, he would hang them on the clothesline on the balcony of his house, which faced ours.

I was convinced that he did this to provoke me, rather than to dry them and save them for the winter season.

As for me, on the rare occasions I caught a small octopus weighing no more than one kilogram—after two or three hours of trying — and even some of them would warn me not to bait "Baby Octopus," because they believed that it was forbidden by law.

However, I ignored the warnings, for the mission I had added to my list of priorities was to catch something and earn points in this unofficial competition, which had been heightened by the gravity and tension of the news my wife brought me, without any ill intent, God forbid:

"Did you see, Ali? Our neighbor hung three octopuses on the rope," or "Wow, I saw our neighbor coming out of the sea holding two in his hands. If only you had seen how people gathered around him..."

And I, determined to preserve my honor — which in my youth was so easily wounded by any remark that doubted my abilities — remained silent, sacrificing my afternoon repose and heading to the sea in the hope of catching a couple and seeing how people would cluster around me, or even hang them on the rope to reclaim my honor, still suspended on the neighbors' clothesline.

We both came from the hill, and neither of us is a "floater" — neither in the sea nor on water, only a splinter high.

Yet, we competed with each other without ever officially declaring it,

And each time he beat me.

And we were friends.

The house where I lived, which has now become my family's property, was only about three meters or less away from the house he rented. We both occupied the second floor, with balconies facing one another. Between the houses lay a shared courtyard where we spent every evening, until late at night, "discussing" the lives of this person and that, the situation in Palestine and Israel, the state of the economy in Greece, and so forth.

Sometimes we would just sit and be content with watching the people returning home or the young ones heading out to enjoy the night.

Every morning, he would go to work the land, while I would head to the sea to swim. At noon, I would return rejuvenated and full of energy, whereas he would come back exhausted. We would meet along the way, wishing each other a pleasant "siesta" or "kalo misimiri" ("good afternoon" in Greek), and he would climb the stairs in heavy, labored steps.

At lunch, we would sometimes exchange plates brimming with love and neighborly goodwill, despite our rivalry. I'd offer him tabbouleh or freekeh, and he would send me labneh made from goat's milk or a large plate of fried mountain snail with rosemary.

Later in the afternoon, when I would awaken from my sleep, I would hear the sound of his tractor's engine signaling that it was headed for his plot to harvest the vegetables that the land had granted him in its bounty.

When he returned, he would bring along okra, tomatoes, cucumbers, and watermelons.

I remember that once, after he had returned and gone up to his house, he stood on his balcony and called out to me (as if he would never call again). I stepped onto my own balcony. I did not see an octopus on the rope, but I saw him carrying a large watermelon in his hands. He asked me to come down and take it, for it was meant for me.

I laughed and said, "Man, toss it to me and I'll catch it. I once worked with watermelons, so I know exactly how it's done."

He asked me if I was sure, and once he calmed down, he tossed it, and it sailed straight into my arms.

I wanted to try him, so I asked him if he could catch it when I tossed it back to him.

He didn't expect that. I tossed it, and he "exploded" in the courtyard where we used to "blow up" our conversations on various topics, one after the other. This time, I triumphed over him, and we burst into laughter.

He went off, of course, and returned with another watermelon—this time having brought it himself without tossing it.

A year and a half ago, in the spring, while he was working his land with his only son, he suffered a heart attack and died.

He was fifty-five when he passed away.

Last summer, I went to find his wife to offer her condolences, and discovered that she had left the rented house and the village.

This morning, on my way back from the shop, I encountered her.

She had returned to the village, rented a new house, and was living in it in style. I found her sitting alone on the threshold of the door adjacent to the street, as is customary among most village widows. She was heavyset, and her many ailments had worsened. From afar, one could discern her black attire and the sorrow in her eyes. She appeared far older than her years.

When she saw me approaching, she stood up, stretched out her arms to greet me, and broke into tears.

I invited her to come to the shared courtyard so that we could all sit together as we used to. At the sound of my invitation, a man wept.

"I can't, Ali... I just can't go there," she said.

I stood with her and we talked for a few minutes about her husband, about fond memories, about watermelons, and other matters.

I asked her about the well-being of her only son, and she told me that this year she was blessed with a grandson.

I smiled and quipped amid the sadness:

"Alright, one out, one in..."

She calmed down a bit, and when I saw a spark in her eyes, I assured her that we would continue our conversation in the shared courtyard.

She shook her head and said:

"It will be alright..."

I bid her farewell and returned home. I climbed the stairs and realized that I, too, had never dared to glance over at the balcony across, throughout all this time. And then I looked.

I saw an empty house, neglected flower pots, and a balcony filled with memories.

I will go to the sea, and when I return, I'll glance at the balcony once more; perhaps I'll see him exhausted, or I might hear the sound of his tractor's engine, or spot a watermelon soaring through the air, or a clothesline laden with octopus.

But I knew that I wouldn't see any of that—only in my memories.

Rest in peace, Vangelis.

Fifty-five years old.

Chapter 18

Katrina

Always clad in her black attire, Katrina sits every evening alone on the same wooden bench on the small port's pier, casting her gaze over the vast, dark sea and the star-laden skies, in search of a sign from Christos, who left this world before his time.

Christos was still regarded as "young" by the islanders and boasted of having an "iron health". Though he grew weary from the sweat-drenched labor in the fields, he always wore a smile.

On that day in August, three years ago, Christos was no longer the cheerful man he had been when he went to the farm to milk the goat; instead, he returned as a silent corpse, dressed in a white shirt and a black suit adorned with a small rose above a heart that continued to love, but had stopped beating.

He was sixty-five when he passed away.

Behind an ornate black Mercedes that was carrying the coffin, walked Angela, the only granddaughter who had not yet reached six, accompanied by her parents and her grandmother, Katrina. Behind them, the villagers trailed, and I was among them.

Angela was very attached to her grandfather, more so than to her parents. For the twenty-four hours before, while the body was still lying in the house wrapped in shrouds, she had sat amidst family and friends, waiting for him to awaken. But he continued to sleep. She called out to him, and when he did not answer, she broke into tears. At the funeral, as she followed the coffin, she called out to him in a loud voice: "Papo... Papo..." But he did not respond, and her wailing grew louder. Since her tears did not soothe her, she suddenly struck the back of the car with all her might using her little hand and shouted in a loud voice that startled everyone, even as tears continued to stream down her cheeks:

"Siku... Papo... Siku!" – "Wake up... Grandpa... wake up!"

But he did not wake up.

Angela's little mind apparently did not register that her grandfather had died, and would no longer accompany her to the beach or teach her how to swim.

Angela's calls to her grandfather touched the hearts of many mourners, and they cried bitter, mournful tears. In that moment, I felt a shudder run through my body. The innocent child's cry still echoes in my mind today, and her image stands before my eyes every time I recall that event or pass by the place where the funeral took place.

As if it left something behind there, and within me. I don't know how others relate to that memory.

But that doesn't matter.

What matters is that a few days after her husband's burial, Katrina discovered that wooden bench and saw in it a warm embrace and a safe haven — perhaps a place to commune with the one whom she loves and is gone. She sits on that bench every day until late at night, silent and lost in thought. Perhaps she tells Christos things she never got the chance to say before, perhaps she apologizes to him for not having cared enough for his health, or maybe she confides personal matters meant for just the two of them. And so she sits for hours on that bench until the village quiets down, the tavern lights go out, and the chairs are gathered around the tables. Then, she rises and returns to her home in heavy, sorrowful steps, while I follow her figure from my balcony overlooking the sea, until it vanishes among the crowded houses.

I knew Katrina well, and I also knew Christos.

Every time this memory rises within me, a surge of envy grips me. I ask myself: "if Angela's cry could reach other places — say, the stars in the skies of this island — even if it did not rouse her grandfather, would it at least stir the long-dead conscience of those many people who feast on the flesh of their brethren, instill terror, and live off extortion, shootings, murder, and the abduction of girls? When will Angela come to us to unleash her cry and pre-empt the cheap death that visits us every day, so that we no longer have to search for a bench to sit upon each evening?"

And there's no guarantee that we will find one.

Siku, people, Siku...

Chapter 19

A Complicated and Simple World

I enter Lod Airport, also known by its Hebrew name "Ben Gurion," and find it half-empty due to the friendly Euro-American air embargo. Some of the passengers were forcibly rerouted onto a flight by the largest "National" airline—, indeed, the only one that dared challenge the missiles and the embargo — and, as a monopoly, its stock price soared.

I pass through all the stations in a surprisingly quiet manner, with no stops, no searches, and no repetitive questions like a parrot. There is something about this that fills me with suspicion, and something that evokes doubt about my own belonging.

In the duty-free area, several TV screens broadcast the same news about missiles fired from Gaza that fell in the south. One of the buildings sustained a direct hit. Around me, there's no chatter, and the tension is evident on everyone's face. I hear no one speak my own language — perhaps out of caution or fear — only silence or the sole official language.

Suddenly, the wail of the alarm siren rings out, warning me and instructing me to seek shelter. Security forces move swiftly and force me to enter a safe zone, perhaps with those who, just last night in Haifa, had demonstrated and wished death upon Arabs with resounding chants and grand slogans.

Our fate is now intertwined: me, death, and whatever lies between us.

I purchase a few essential summer garments at the clothing store, disregarding shouts for an ethnic boycott, as if we had reverted to division based on national belonging rather than on opinions.

A young man greets me, formally and with a sullen expression, looking like he's trying to keep his distance—and I sense that he hopes I will withdraw as quickly as possible to protect myself, and perhaps him too. Our exchange is brief and matter-of-fact... Long minutes pass until my son finishes choosing his summer clothes and the sports shoes that suit him... For a moment, the young man forgets the situation, interjects in my conversation, and tells me that my son's bag bearing the "Real Madrid" emblem is most excellent. I ask him what he means, and he replies that he is an ardent supporter of Real Madrid, whereas his sister is an equally passionate Barcelona fan. He adds that he gets annoyed with her during the Clásico and they quarrel, but by the next morning, they reconcile and resume their fraternal relations.

I favor him with an understanding smile, for the pattern is similar at my home. My son and I — He taunts me with Real, and I tease him with Messi.

I sympathize with his sister, and he with my son.

And the war over Gaza continues.

Death continues to reap its harvest, far from both Barcelona and Madrid.

This world is strange in its simplicity...

Chapter 20

Farewell, Eliki Christaki

Twenty-nine years ago, she presented herself to me.

She never inquired about my origins, my family background, my religion, nationality, race, skin color, or even my demeanor. She loved me as I am, right from our first meeting. Or, more accurately, she loved everyone that way.

Every morning, she would bring me country eggs and fresh goat milk from her modest farm in the small village on the island of Crete.

I remember that once, I returned a bottle of milk to our neighbor Rola — the proprietor of the nearby shop where I bought it— and brought me a pot full of boiling country goat milk to put in the fridge.

"Shame on you, Ali. Buying milk when you're at our place? Everything you want is already at home!" she said, in the direct manner of the villagers.

Every summer, I would meet her. Her smile never left her lips as she, discreetly and with a hint of mischief, "so that the old man (her husband) wouldn't see," would bring a portion of her meal for the cats at home, while adding the leftover food from the farm.

Six years ago, she was diagnosed with the disease, "the one whose name is not mentioned." The cancer in her lungs and bones was at an advanced stage, and the doctors doubted the benefit of treatment, estimating that she would live for at most six months.

She defied science, the disease, and everyone, and continued to tend every day to the potted flowers in the courtyard. When she could, she would go to the farm, returning in pain and complaining about the filth there and the condition of her cats, chickens, and rabbits.

A year after the disease was discovered, I developed facial nerve paralysis (facialis). I struggled to see myself in the mirror, and I was in low spirits.

One evening, we sat together, and she asked me:

"How are you, Ali?"

I knew just how much she loved me, so I opened up my heart to her and shared my feelings. Without hesitation, she raised her index finger at me with a determined, maternal, and loving resolve and said:

"Thank God, Ali, thank God."

I do not know where that strength came from, that entered directly into my heart and revived it.

Nevertheless, I was embarrassed by the comparison between my health and hers.

This summer, she waited for us to come to her.

Yesterday, she laughed and ate her favorite vanilla ice cream, and this morning she left us.

Her body, wrapped in shrouds, was laid out in the living room, and everyone sat around it, sharing memories of her parades, her stories, and her adventures, after she had given birth to her eldest daughter, who had not yet reached sixteen.

May God have mercy on you, my wife's grandmother, who was like a second mother to me, my summer mother.

Farewell, Eliki Christaki.

Chapter 21

His name was Mathios

He asked me to accompany him to the small kitchen in the tavern he ran, which was located on the ground floor beneath our house in a small village on an island whose population did not exceed a few hundred.

I remember that the sea looked strange and marvelous that evening. Waves, unlike any I had seen before, struck the rocks that guarded the house, and splashes of water reached all the way to the balcony of the modest country inn on the second floor.

We entered the kitchen, and he opened an old cupboard in which the maps of the tavern's tables were laid out. He slid one of them aside and produced a large weapon hidden among them. He examined it closely, as if it were his beloved, and then tossed it into my hands.

Throughout my life, I had never touched a weapon and knew only of a pistol and a rifle — and even that only from movies. My hands trembled under the weight of the responsibility it imposed on me. The weapon was heavy, over a meter in length, and its middle section was like a tube with a diameter wider than the rest, pierced by many holes.

"What is this?" I asked him in English as I tried to get rid of it and return it to him.

"Kalo (is it good)?" he replied in Greek with a questioning tone while smiling, "Take it with you if you want. You need it in Palestine. On the mountain, in the banana greenhouse, I have two crates full of bullets."

His name was Mathios. He was in his fifties when I set foot on the soil of Crete in one of the summers of the mid-eighties. At that time, I was a young student beginning my journey at Moscow State University.

Mathios was a tall man with a stooped back, a strong voice, a long white mustache, and long hair, which he tended with what little remained of it and tied into a small braid.

He was an educated, broad-minded man who read widely and loved philosophy; an upright soul who despised concessions or compromising solutions — a "pursuer of justice" par excellence. He was a temperamental man, and more than once I saw him shouting at a few pestering customers, or closing the tavern and leaving the patrons seated outside at the tables without paying for what they had taken.

Perhaps that was the reason he lived alone.

When he listened to the news about the invasion of Lebanon in the early eighties, his heart would grow heavy, and he would speak proudly of the RPG-bearing children.

He did not know English, and I did not know Greek, but we understood each other through gestures and, above all, the language of the heart.

My stay there lasted for over a month. Due to our proximity, and to fill the free time I had after returning from the sea, I would help him with the running of the tavern — especially in serving the foreign tourists among the customers — even without him asking. When I refused to accept the money he offered in exchange for this service, he always found a clever way to give it to me.

At night, I would sit on the balcony on the second floor, directly above him, and watch him. He would close the tavern after the last of the visitors had left, turn off the lights, and sit alone at a table near the sea for an hour or more, drinking a glass of whiskey, smoking a pipe, and gazing at the twinkling stars above the dark sea, or checking how many days remained until the full moon appeared. Then he would go to his house.

Alone.

Nothing awaited him there except loneliness and silence.

Many times I followed him as he walked, and many times I wondered about his life.

After a while, when the tavern was closed, he moved to live in his small house next to the "two crates of bullets" by the banana greenhouse, a walk of half an hour or more away.

Every summer vacation, I would meet him on my way twice, and sometimes more. In the morning, when I sat on the balcony overlooking the beach, I would see him in the distance walking to do some shopping at the village store and to check on the condition of the fish in the boats returning from the sea.

Each summer, I noticed the wear of years and solitude on his body, yet he always kept his smile and asked about the situation in Palestine.

He took a keen interest in our situation with the utmost sincerity and seriousness.

I had a special regard for him. In my eyes, he was self-taught, a patriot, a kind human being, an altruist, generous, and full of self-respect.

That summer, I did not see him.

I knew he was dead.

This man is gone, and he will never again come on foot to the village every morning.

Rest in peace, Mathios.

You lived and died alone, and I can only hope that was your choice.

You have gone,

Your beautiful memory remains,

and the Kalashnikov remains.

You have no idea how calm I feel, because you have no idea how many of his we now have in our hands.

If you had known which side he was aligned with, you would not have asked me to accompany you all to the kitchen.

Bibliography

1. The website of the Israel Hypnosis Association www.hypno.co.il ↥
2. Thomas, K. B. (1987): General practice consultations: is there any point in being positive? British Medical Journal vol. 294, pp. 1201-1203 ↥
3. Emoto, M. (1999): "Messages from Water", Hado Kyoiku Sha Co., Ltd. ↥
4. Pascual-Leone A, Nguyet D, Cohen LG, Brasil-Neto JP, Cammarota A, Hallett M. 1995. Modulation of muscle responses evoked by transcranial magnetic stimulation during the acquisition of new fine motor skills. J. Neurophysiology. 74: 1037–45 ↥
5. Al-Fatiha – the first chapter of the Qur'an recited in every prayer and various circumstances in the daily life of a Muslim. ↥
6. Al-Hajjaj bin Yusuf (714-660) – governor of Iraq during the Umayyad period. ↥
7. Hadith – things transmitted from the Prophet Muhammad or about him. ↥
8. Happy. ↥
9. Out of transparency and in the spirit of partnership — and to ensure continuity and professionalism in the treatment — I wish to note that after obtaining my degree and returning to my country, I held several additional sessions with Dr. Ayman to continue treatment of the issues that had initially arisen, which were postponed until after his studies were completed. ↥
10. It is clear that Rana's story is complex, and that the treatment did not end here. I have included this excerpt solely to illustrate the hypnotherapy method I used to tackle

a recurring bad dream. And not only that, of course. I already mentioned in the first part of the book that hypnotherapy and dreams have much in common, since it is possible through hypnosis to pause a specific dream and treat it as I did here with Rana. The discussion here is not about explaining the dream or its symbols, but merely referring to it as it is — a single entity — without delving into details for its understanding. ↥

www.ingramcontent.com/pod-product-compliance
Lightning Source LLC
LaVergne TN
LVHW100305210926
848480LV00003B/1025
9798900011981